RAVES FOR
MY EX-WIFE'S WEDDING DRESS

"A truly hilarious idea. An idea so mischievously zany that, once unveiled, it sparked interest and support from hundreds of thousands of people across the globe in fewer than three weeks—demonstrating the awesome power, and potential perils, of letting the world in on your personal life via the Internet." —*Today*

> "When [Cotter's ex-wife] told him to do what he liked with the gown, he did just that, coming up with 101 awesome and creative uses for it." —**The Huffington Post**

"Kevin has made great effort to start cataloging the humorous ways in which one could possibly reuse a wedding dress around the home. Obviously, none of them is very conventional, but that's what makes it fun. Finding uses for the dress and the process of writing a blog are an unusual yet practical way to cope with his loss as his humor is frequently mixed with thoughts of being a newly single father. It's therapeutic and cathartic in its own right, and we're glad that it's being done with humor and a side of creativity. When life gives you lemons (or a wedding dress), you floss your teeth with it and let the good times roll." —**Apartment Therapy**

> "Cotter's blog, My Ex-Wife's Wedding Dress, has become a viral phenomenon, showing him using that white lace gown for everything from flossing his teeth and straining spaghetti to making a yoga mat and dressing a scarecrow (complete with Darth Vader mask)." —**AOL News**

continued . . .

"Kevin is now becoming an international star for turning the dress into everything from a piece of floss to a Darth Vader scarecrow to a pasta strainer....Expect this blog to be turned into a romantic comedy starring Jason Bateman by next summer." —Dlisted

"Kevin started a hilarious Web site and asked the users to help him come up with 101 uses for the dress. Well, Kevin has blown up. He's since done interviews for *ABC Nightly News* and AOL." —**The Chive**

"Impressively, he's heartbreakingly honest about how difficult divorce can be....What I find so fascinating is how he's using the dress as a way to really home in on some of his feelings in the year after his divorce. It's kind of poetic, really. At the end of the experiment, he'll have a tattered, torn, stained piece of fabric—I'm sure how the end of the marriage and the messy pulling apart felt. But then he can get rid of it and, hopefully, move on. Personally, I'd read his book." —Redbook

"A jilted husband has exacted hilarious revenge on the wife who dumped him by becoming an Internet sensation with ingenious ways of using her wedding dress." —*Daily Mail* (UK)

"I must say he's very creative and has created a very funny Web site....You must see this for yourself....Cotter has gotten a whole lot of publicity—I'm talking worldwide—on the blog site." —Gather.com

"While we're personally fans of the scarecrow, Cotter has also used the gown for a drip cloth when he changes the oil in his Honda Element and a gas cap. Hilarity ensues." —**Autoblog.com**

101
USES FOR MY
EX-WIFE'S
WEDDING
DRESS

KEVIN COTTER

NEW
AMERICAN
LIBRARY

NEW AMERICAN LIBRARY
Published by New American Library, a division of Penguin Group (USA) Inc., 375 Hudson Street,
New York, New York 10014, USA
Penguin Group (Canada), 90 Eglinton Avenue East, Suite 700, Toronto, Ontario M4P 2Y3, Canada
(a division of Pearson Penguin Canada Inc.)
Penguin Books Ltd., 80 Strand, London WC2R 0RL, England
Penguin Ireland, 25 St. Stephen's Green, Dublin 2, Ireland (a division of Penguin Books Ltd.)
Penguin Group (Australia), 250 Camberwell Road, Camberwell, Victoria 3124, Australia
(a division of Pearson Australia Group Pty. Ltd.)
Penguin Books India Pvt. Ltd., 11 Community Centre, Panchsheel Park, New Delhi - 110 017, India
Penguin Group (NZ), 67 Apollo Drive, Rosedale, Auckland 0632, New Zealand
(a division of Pearson New Zealand Ltd.)
Penguin Books (South Africa) (Pty.) Ltd., 24 Sturdee Avenue, Rosebank, Johannesburg 2196, South Africa

Penguin Books Ltd., Registered Offices:
80 Strand, London WC2R 0RL, England

First published by New American Library,
a division of Penguin Group (USA) Inc.

First Printing, November 2011
10 9 8 7 6 5 4 3 2 1

REGISTERED TRADEMARK—MARCA REGISTRADA

LIBRARY OF CONGRESS CATALOGING-IN-PUBLICATION DATA:
Cotter, Kevin.
101 uses for my ex-wife's wedding dress/Kevin Cotter.
p. cm.
ISBN 978-0-451-23589-3
1. Divorce—Humor. 2. Wives—Humor. I. Title.
PN6231.D662C68 2011
818'.602—dc23   2011024542

Set in Univers
Designed by Pauline Neuwirth

Printed in China

Contents

<

3 I Am a Domestic God   41

4 The Mancave   61

5 I Am a Manly Man   79

vi

vii

CONTENTS

ix

101
USES FOR MY
EX-WIFE'S
WEDDING
DRESS

Big Business

LET'S JUST START with a couple of comments about the typical wedding. The wedding industry in the United States is now estimated to be a $40 *billion* empire. It's mind-blowing, isn't it? But the idea of weddings as big business isn't entirely new. Okay, hundreds of years ago wives were snatched by men from neighboring tribes and brought home to spend their days literally barefoot and pregnant. But later wives were purchased in exchange for cattle. Can you imagine what those marital spats were like? "I gave up my best milker and for what? So that I could come home to eat this crap?" The Romans were the big liberals who decided that women could actually have the right to choose whether to marry. But even after that, marriages were often politically driven and used as a way of creating alliances between kingdoms. But still, that's a far cry from what weddings today have become. Between jewelers, reception venues, caterers, and tuxedo specialists, and six thousand bridal shows a year, there is a lot of dough being splashed out on a single day. At least, as I'm about to show you, the wedding dress can be brought home and put to work after the musicians have packed up and the champagne bottles have been drunk dry.

→

Introduction

"EXCUSE ME, SIR, but we don't allow pets in the store," said the smirking Starbucks barista from behind the counter. I had stopped in for a rare $3 cup of Joe. Not that it is unusual to find me drinking coffee or for them to be serving pricey brew, but for a frugal guy like me, it was an uncommon indulgence.

"Nothing alive up there. It's just my ex-wife's wedding dress. I'm using it today as a turban," I reassured her, not remotely surprised by her reaction.

I couldn't blame her for her confusion. At this point the once pristine white dress had been used for more than a few applications—some of them very simple (like a towel or window curtain), others totally outrageous. The dress was looking pretty scruffy and probably could be mistaken for an animal by now. And by this point my brother, Colin, and I were used to the double takes, the stares, and the whispers. Together, and with the support and ideas of many people both far and near, we had been working to document my goal of finding 101 unconventional uses for my ex-wife's wedding dress.

Am I insane? No. And I can back that up with a statement from my therapist. No, I didn't snap when my ex-wife dumped me two years ago. I'm just an ordinary guy who found an unusual way of working through a very challenging time. How did I get here? I'll tell you.

On July 5, 2009, my wife of twelve years announced that she was leaving me. It wasn't a complete surprise, as I knew things hadn't been going well, but the actual split was as raw and painful as it could be. This was a loss like nothing I had ever experienced. After all, we'd been together for more than half my life. As she cleared away her belongings, I realized that she had left just one thing in her side of the closet: a giant white box marked "To Have and To Hold." It was her wedding dress, sitting in its preservation box, positioned smack in the center of the middle shelf.

"You left something," I told her.

"What's that?" she asked.

"Your wedding dress," I explained.

"I'm not taking *that*," she answered.

"Well, I don't want it. What do you expect me to do with it?" I lamented.

"Whatever the *&#$ you want," she replied.

When my wife walked out after almost two decades together, she left a thirty-five-year-old father of two with no experience being an adult on his own. We'd been together since high school and suddenly we were no more. Of course, I wasn't without my blessings; I had my house, my kids, my job, my family and friends, and my Honda Element. Oh, and my ex-wife's wedding dress.

For a long while, the dress just stayed in the closet, staring at me from its perch. I didn't tell anyone at first that my wife had not only left me but also her dress. After all, it was sort of awkward and embarrassing. Like she was really trying to drive home a point about what she thought of our relationship. When I finally confessed to my family over dinner one night (one of the perks of a fresh divorce is free meals) that the dress was mine and I had no idea what I should do with it, well, the suggestions were immediate and forthcoming, generally in the form of a toilet paper substitution. Offhandedly my sister-in-law, Jenny, commented that there must be 101 uses for a wedding dress. Click. The wheels in my head started turning. Could the wedding dress possibly be used 101 different ways? The idea struck me as ridiculously funny and possibly therapeutic as well. I've always thought spending an obscene amount of money on something that would only be worn once was kind of stupid, even more so now in light of what had happened. Maybe I could get some practical use out of it and give it back its value. I wasn't sure how my ex-wife would feel if I used her old dress as a doormat, but I'd deal with that later. So I began collecting ideas and suggestions from family and friends, and before I knew it I had a list of over a hundred possible uses for my ex-wife's wedding dress. It was time for action.

My little brother, Colin, and I set about going down the list and taking some photographs. Colin's a great person and was a huge support to me during these tough early few months. That said, the guy's no Ansel Adams. I estimated we'd need about a thousand shots to get one or two usable ones. Regardless, my collection of funny (at least to me) photographs started growing and I began to wonder if there was a way for me to share my crazy pictures as a sort of pick-me-up for others who were in a similar situation. After all, who hasn't been dumped at one point or another? I'm well aware that I'm not the first person in history to be devastated by a divorce and had to face all the challenges that come with starting over. My situation isn't all that unusual. I just did something unusual with my situation.

Enter the Internet. Maybe it was once a giant top secret Pentagon project, but now it was a way to share my story with the world. I'm not a computer guy. I'm a salesman by trade. But I do have some friends with computer skills, and before I knew it I went from a guy who barely knew what a blog was to a man who runs a Web site with an international following and who has appeared on TV and radio programs around the world. Even the *National Enquirer* gave me a feature (I'm secretly extremely proud of this one).

I'm Kevin Cotter. I'm a father, a son, a brother, an uncle, and a friend. I am a loyal Honda owner. I like steak. My favorite store is Target. I'm a runner and an athlete. But I'm not afraid to put on women's clothing. I'm a box salesman with an irrational fear of glitter. And I'm the owner of one very used wedding dress. This is my story.

Who's Kevin Cotter?
And What's Tulle?

1

AGAIN, I'M JUST an ordinary guy. When this all started, I had no idea where it would lead. When my wife left me, I simply didn't know what to do with her wedding dress. I really didn't want it. Walking by my empty closet several times a day and seeing that big box just sitting there was indescribably painful. But in my darkness I had found something that I thought was hilarious. What could I really do with this symbol of my former life? I knew it would work as a towel or a drop cloth, but would it hold up to some of the crazier applications? Would I even get away with trying? Would I get arrested or possibly killed at some point? I started to think that the concept of unconventional uses for a very conventional piece of bridal wear was very funny. I still do. But in the beginning, I wasn't familiar with women's formal wear. I was barely capable of finding clothes at Target for my daughter. (Which I still get wrong. Every time.) I didn't know a thing about a wedding dress. I didn't even know the proper names for its various parts. And the thing was huge. I mean *huge*. At first I really had no plan. But once the idea of finding everyday uses for a used bit of formal wear took hold, I was hooked. I could, and I would, find 101 uses for my ex-wife's wedding dress.

I suppose at this point it might be helpful to give you a little more background on the guy who found himself walking around town with a wedding dress on his head. Who is Kevin Cotter? How did all this happen? Well, I'll tell you.

DRESS USE #1: **WINTER SCARF**

A wedding dress makes a great scarf in chilly weather. For someone like me, it's a more practical solution than having a bunch of winter wear that I barely use taking up extra space in my closet.

I HAVE LIVED IN TUCSON, ARIZONA, MY ENTIRE LIFE. My family lives here. I have no intention of leaving Tucson. That said, my lifelong dream is to be an anti-snowbird. Is that the right term? A snowbird is what we call the people from up North who winter in Arizona. I want to go the opposite direction when Tucson starts to boil. So I wonder what you call someone who summers where it is colder? Well, whatever you call those people—that is what I aspire to be. People in Tucson get really cranky by August. Of course, the winters don't get that cold, although we usually have a handful of nights when the temperature drops below freezing. All in all, though, I'm pretty content out here in the desert.

101 USES FOR MY EX-WIFE'S WEDDING DRESS

WASHCLOTH

A wedding dress makes a great washcloth because the mesh lining allows for gentle exfoliation while the silky parts are gentle enough for a thorough scrubbing.

AS I'VE MENTIONED, I SELL BOXES. As a young boy, I dreamed of being either an FBI agent, a firefighter, or a box salesman. The first two options ultimately seemed a bit drab for me, which is why I have been busy peddling paper and plastic products for the last thirteen-plus years. Why do I do it? The adrenaline rush may seem the obvious answer, but you might not be aware of the perks. What do regular folks do when they need a big box for their kids to play in? I just bring one home from the office. And bubble wrap and tape? Well, I'm everybody's best buddy at moving time. No, I'm never scrambling for a plastic bag to throw my dirty soccer cleats into or a piece of paper to jot down a hot chick's phone number. Those things just go with the job. I know you're jealous. Who wouldn't be?

101 USES FOR MY EX-WIFE'S WEDDING DRESS

SPORTING EVENT BANNER

Don't know how to show your favorite team your support? Consider a wedding dress sports banner. A couple of Magic Markers and a little creativity and there you go. I do believe we played a large role in the Wildcats' big win that day.

AS I FIRST BEGAN TO CONSIDER USES FOR MY EX-WIFE'S WEDDING DRESS, I DECIDED THAT ANY PROPOSAL THAT INVOLVED CUTTING UP THE DRESS WOULD DESTROY ITS INTEGRITY. After all, a cut-up wedding dress is just a bunch of fabric. I also needed to start with the "manliest" suggestions, because I wanted to appear as tough as possible while running around with my ex-wife's wedding dress. Not only that, but I'm pretty no-nonsense, so the dress was going to have to work its way into my everyday life, at least in the beginning. I should warn you, the practicalities of taking a giant white wedding dress out in public for a project like this are a little more involved than you might imagine. Carrying a backpack full of wedding dress into the sports stadium got us stopped by security. It was only a quick mind and a fast tongue that convinced the confused guard that a wedding dress was not as dangerous to the crowd as, say, loaded weaponry. However, he did confiscate the actual sack we were using to carry it to our seats.

PASTA STRAINER

As a pasta strainer, a wedding dress with a layer of tulle works wonderfully.

WHEN YOU FIND YOURSELF THE OWNER OF A GENTLY USED WED-
DING DRESS, IT IS IMPORTANT TO ALSO LEARN THE TECHNICAL
TERMS FOR ITS VARIOUS LAYERS. I thought the inner layers of the
dress would make a great pasta strainer for my SpongeBob SquarePants
macaroni. However, on my blog I mistakenly referred to the material used
as *mesh*. I was immediately corrected. It is *tulle*. Tulle, according to *Mer-
riam-Webster*, is a "sheer, often stiffened silk, rayon, or nylon net." The
word hails from the French, after the city of Tulle, where tulle was first
manufactured. I am now very clear on the definition of tulle. If you are
lucky enough to get your hands on a used wedding dress, hopefully it will
come with yards of this very handy material.

TOWEL

A wedding dress actually makes a terrible towel. It may look nice but it is simply not effective. It doesn't absorb.

THERE MAY BE A LOT OF USES FOR A WEDDING DRESS, BUT A WED-
DING DRESS IS NOT NECESSARILY SUITED FOR EVERY USE. As you'll
soon learn, flossing your teeth with a ball gown is painful. I can attest to
that. Then again, it is a perfect grill cover. Any application that involved
me wearing the dress was always difficult. Although the dress was *huge*,
squeezing a vital specimen of masculinity like me into the actual bodice
(yes, I know what a bodice is—now anyway) was nearly impossible. On
its first unveiling while camping, I did manage to get it over my head, but
that was about it. And then there was the issue of the miniature replica
dress that my ex also left behind. That's right. I not only have her wedding
dress, I have a doll-size version of it as well.

DRESS USE #6: # SHOWER CURTAIN

On the other hand, a wedding dress makes an excellent shower curtain. Because of the holes in the edging, it attaches easily to a curtain rod. It's not waterproof, but that isn't an issue for me. I take short showers, in preparation for the day when Tucson runs out of water.

WHEN I STARTED MY WEB SITE, WWW.MYEXWIFESWEDDINGDRESS. COM, I DIDN'T TRULY UNDERSTAND THE POWER OF THE INTERNET. Within days of launching my site, I had a few hundred followers. Six days later I had twenty-five thousand visitors. Two days after that, seventy-five thousand *in one day.* Shortly thereafter, radio and television interview requests, and e-mails from movie producers and reporters from newspapers and magazines around the world started pouring in. My phone was ringing at all hours. People all over the world were watching my story. For a regular guy from Arizona, it wasn't something I was really prepared for. Curiously, I have a very large following in the Netherlands. I'm not quite sure what is going on over there.

TOILET *AND* SHOWER MAT

If you have Pergo flooring in your bathroom too, then you know that water is not good for Pergo. A wedding dress is a good way to prolong the life of your tiles. It can function as either an attractive shower or toilet mat. Anytime a wedding dress can multitask, I feel really, really good.

I'M NOT A WRITER BY TRADE. I'm a carton expert. I work in sales for a Tucson box company. When I'm not peddling paper or trying to understand how to buy clothes for my daughter, I'm usually fishing or camping somewhere. I am an accidental author, but if my story can help someone else through a dark time, then it's worth the struggle to put my tale down into words. I work on the other side of this industry, making sure that the paper needed for those printing presses arrives in good condition and on time. Sitting on this side of the equation feels a little funny. For example, the semicolon confounds me. I don't understand it; it feels as if a comma or a period could always replace it. See.

DRESSING FOR YOUR SPECIAL DAY

As I've said, it's important to understand the construction of a typical wedding dress before putting it to work around your house or yard. Actually, I believe that when choosing a wedding dress, a bride should be mindful of how her decisions will impact use of the dress later on. For example, spaghetti straps could be so useful in so many ways. When selecting a bodice, I feel that a corset style could be somewhat limiting and give the dress an artificial stiffness or unwanted height when using it as a towel or rug. The type of silhouette decided on also affects how much material you'll have to work with. For example, a good basic A-line should give you plenty of fabric, but a mermaid style might be difficult to fit over a man or a scarecrow. Of course, if we're simply talking yards of cloth, then you can always make it up by choosing a Cathedral train, which extends seven feet from the waist. In my expert opinion, that really should be enough for the majority of applications. If you think you might want to water-ski behind the dress one day, though, then I would recommend getting a ten-foot royal train. Final consideration should be given to the presence of tulle, which is invaluable for so many uses. Flowers and bows are also nice additions—say, for cake decorating or wrapping gifts. And don't get me started on things like gloves, headpieces, and shrugs.

Survival

2

I IMAGINE THAT most breakups aren't a complete shock to either of the involved parties. I'll admit that things were rocky. I wasn't exactly blindsided. But even so, the actual split was unbelievably painful. I had so many questions: How would my children cope? Would their little lives be forever tainted? How would my family react? Would life ever return to normal, and if so, when? I can best describe myself at that time as "lost." I don't remember exactly how much time I took off from work. Being a box salesman requires visiting customers and putting on a happy face, and I simply didn't have it in me. I take my work performance very seriously, but other than keeping up with e-mails, I was miserably unproductive. As for home, well, who could have imagined that the sound of SpongeBob SquarePants singing from his residence down in Bikini Bottom would be something I would miss? Believe me, it has nothing to do with bikinis. Yet I found myself longing for those days when my house sounded like a *home*. I used to look forward to those rare moments when my wife and kids were out and I could read a fly-fishing magazine or watch a football game without interruption. But now the silence left me replaying the events of the last few years and wondering how everything I knew had simply fallen apart.

The first few months after any breakup are just about getting through the day. There are a lot of hours between sunrise and sundown that need to be filled. When rattling around your now-empty house, or struggling to keep yourself clean and fed, a wedding dress can actually prove mighty handy.

DRESS USE #8: **FOOTREST**

A preserved wedding dress in its box makes a perfect footrest. There's still room for your remote control, plus, there is no need for a coaster under your beer. And no one nagging you to use one.

AFTER ONLY SIX YEARS OF COLLEGE, I WAS AWARDED A BACHELOR'S DEGREE IN GENERAL BUSINESS. What set me apart from my fellow graduates was the emphasis in Spanish. With this highly specialized combination, I set my sights high and eventually landed my dream job. As you are now well aware, I'm a box salesman. Okay, technically I sell "cartons," which everyone knows is the correct term for a corrugated container. Not just that, I sell bags, tape, bubble wrap, labels, and more. I think this makes me a packaging expert. As painful as it was, I kept walking past that box in the closet trying to invite the pain, thinking that maybe having it hurt a whole lot all at once would make my recovery start sooner, like ripping off a Band-Aid. Unfortunately there is no quick and easy way to move on. I was going to have to let time heal my wounds, as the saying goes. That said, once I got used to having my ex-wife's wedding dress in the house, I began to really admire its packaging. My professional opinion is that this was one of the finest boxes I had ever seen. And I bet it cost far more than any box *I* ever sold. What a racket. First you pay for a high-priced gown, which you will wear exactly once. Then you have to pay a preservation specialist to put it in a special box, where it will do nothing but sit there, occupying precious shelf space for a lifetime.

101 USES FOR MY EX-WIFE'S WEDDING DRESS

BEANBAG

There are lots of perks that come along with being a box salesman. I'm never scrambling for a pen or a piece of paper. But another perk I'd never realized was the availability of scrap foam. A wedding dress stuffed with bits of urethane makes a really comfortable place to sit, especially if you're chatting on the phone.

I GREW UP CATHOLIC. Like "my-father-used-to-be-a-priest" kind of Catholic. I'm dead serious. PhD in Canon Law and everything. Okay, he did leave the church to marry my mother, but my family is truly, intensely Catholic. So you can imagine my delight and anticipation at announcing my impending divorce to my family. I was incredibly nervous driving to my parents' house that first time after my ex-wife left, afraid that I had let everyone down. I felt like a failure, to be honest. However, instead of the disappointment I'd expected, my family gathered around me and gave me nothing but love and support during what was a very difficult time. My mom and dad said I could call anytime. And I did. Although I usually tried to wait until at least five thirty in the morning, which was the earliest I really felt comfortable waking them.

101 USES FOR MY EX-WIFE'S WEDDING DRESS

DRESS USE #10: **FLYSWATTER**

With such a deep hatred of houseflies, you can imagine my disappointment when I learned that a wedding dress makes only a so-so flyswatter. Apparently those thousands of lenses, giving them a 360-degree visual field, make sneaking up behind the little buggers with a giant white dress quite difficult.

I'M NOT JUST A SALESMAN OR A GUY WHO ONLY OWNS HONDAS OR A LOVER OF RED MEAT. I'm also a Sudoku puzzle champion. And a self-proclaimed Ninja fly killer, known to catch them midair. There are two things I hate: glitter and houseflies. Houseflies are obvious. They're dirty. I'm not. Glitter, however, might need explaining. Confetti implies an element of celebration and can be easily vacuumed up or swept into a dustpan. Sequins suggest formal wear, which isn't really my style, but I don't mind seeing them on an attractive lady. Their little sister, Glitter, however, lacks any real purpose. She just flashes unexpectedly and sticks to everything. You can't escape her. She's like wildly gay sand. And, truth be told, I have a sand phobia as well.

If you find yourself needing a tissue, I can tell you that a silky wedding dress feels really nice on a runny nose. My ex-wife's wedding dress gave me the nicest nose-blowing experience of my life. However, satin is not highly absorbent and you'll be needing a lot of material if you want to save on buying tissues. Assuming you're not in the paper business, like I am.

I'M NOT A GUY WHO SHOWS A LOT OF EMOTION, BUT THE AFTERMATH OF A DIVORCE IS HARD ON EVERYONE. I was particularly worried about my kids, although I'll admit that having their parents separate actually helped them to fit in *better* at school. The day my daughter told me that she was now part of the majority group in her class was a sad commentary on our society, I thought. The first few months were confusing for them, shuffling back and forth between their parents and not having any real routine to speak of. When parents separate, many kids cling to the hope that the situation is just temporary and Mom and Dad will be reuniting soon. I wasn't sure how to handle this and turned to some books on the subject. The expert advice is basically to firmly and consistently crush their little wishes and dreams at every turn. Nice.

31

DRESS USE #12: **PUNCHING BAG**

A wedding dress punching bag isn't difficult to set up and could be really helpful in relieving stress during the early days after a relationship collapses. All you need is a couple of sleeping bags to stuff into the dress and some duct tape. I hung it from my garage door opener and started punching away.

I NEVER HAD TROUBLE SLEEPING BEFORE MY EX-WIFE WALKED OUT, BUT SUDDENLY I BEGAN TO SUFFER FROM TERRIBLE INSOMNIA, ESPECIALLY ON THOSE EVENINGS WHEN I WAS HOME ALONE. On the nights my kids weren't there, I would purposely stay up well past my formerly strict 10.00 p.m. bedtime hoping that I could become tired enough to finally fall asleep. When I did it was only to wake suddenly, my whole body shaking. Exhausted, I turned to pharmaceuticals. Ambien became my new best friend. However, I must have the metabolism of a little girl, because all I needed was one-fourth of a pill to work its magic. The first night I popped a whole pill and sat at the computer, waiting for medical magic. I found myself the next morning in bed, but how I got there was a mystery. At least I was rested enough to quickly check that I hadn't gone sending my ex any cathartic e-mails.

A wedding dress actually makes a very good bib, despite its poor absorbency. Which is useful if you require sleeping pills and have a tendency to drool. Or if you just want to treat yourself to a manly meal of hot wings.

I HAVE TO ADMIT THAT I'M SELFISHLY SO THANKFUL THAT MY CHIL-
DREN ARE OLD ENOUGH TO BE PRETTY INDEPENDENT WHEN IT
COMES TO THINGS LIKE GETTING FOOD INTO THEIR MOUTHS AND
USING THE TOILET. Single parenting is hard enough for me, and I'm sure
I wouldn't be coping as well if I had a toddler or newborn to care for. But
in my reading about children and divorce I learned that smaller children
have an easier time adjusting when parents part ways. The younger they
are, the fewer—if any—memories they have of Mom and Dad being together. Maybe if I'd had a crystal ball and knew what was coming, I would
have preferred the split to have happened earlier to make it all easier on
them. And there would have been all sorts of ways in which a wedding
dress could have helped me: playpen, changing table, crib mobile. But I
do recognize that it would still have been very difficult, dress or no dress.

Buying the clothes is only half the battle. You then have to keep them clean. I hate, hate, hate doing laundry. However, the task is made slightly more enjoyable when using my ex-wife's dress as a means of transporting my dirty clothes. A wedding dress actually makes a fantastic laundry bag, assuming you didn't just use it as an oil pan.

I SUGGESTED AT ONE POINT TO MY EX-WIFE THAT WE SHOULD EXCHANGE OUR CHILDREN NAKED. It would put a clear end to the complaining that all the clothes *she* bought for the kids were ending up at my house, although I was quick to point out that this did work both ways. I was out there, braving the world of frills and lace, too, you know. Nothing is more frightful to a newly single dad than the girls' clothing section at Target. A root canal would be less painful. My son's clothes are easy; they're just smaller versions of my own. So it's got a little stain on it? He doesn't mind. Girly clothing, on the other hand, is beyond my comprehension. When I shop for my daughter I rarely get it right. And forget laundry. Some items need hanging, others can be folded. Some shirts actually come in two pieces. I was completely lost and remain so to this day.

DRESS USE #15: GROCERY BAG

A wedding dress makes an excellent and eco-friendly reusable grocery bag, which can easily be slung over your shoulder and carried out to your car. I mean, you can't really get greener than that.

DURING THOSE FIRST MONTHS, SPENDING TIME WITH MY BROTHER WORKING ON A LIST OF 101 USES FOR MY EX-WIFE'S WEDDING DRESS AND THEN STAGING OUR SHOTS WAS A MUCH-NEEDED BREAK FROM THE DAY-TO-DAY STRUGGLL OF FINDING MY WAY POST-DIVORCE. Let me tell you something. Taking a wedding dress out into public requires a backbone. Some people thought my adventure was hilarious; others were horrified, accusing me of disrespecting my ex and our marriage. That wasn't my intention at all. This was about healing myself and helping others going through the same experience with laughter. However, not everyone saw it that way.

Standing in the supermarket one day, an elderly woman in front of me asked why, exactly, did I have a wedding dress lining my shopping cart. I explained that my ex-wife's dress was acting as an eco-friendly reusable shopping bag. With horror she exclaimed, "Why, that's awful, just *awful*, to use your wife's dress that way!" I clarified: "Ex. Ex-wife. She left me. And she left the dress."

"Then you just keep using that dress, honey," my checkout companion exclaimed with conviction, patting my arm like she was my grandmother.

IF YOU WERE STUCK ON A DESERT ISLAND . . .

Just in case you aren't yet convinced that a wedding dress can be helpful and so versatile, allow me to compare the many ways in which a used bridal gown could be of real use to you if you were stranded in the woods or hiding out in a nuclear fallout shelter. I'll make it simple for you: my ex-wife's wedding dress versus the Swiss Army knife.

Dress uses: hammock, canopy, towel, dental floss, fishing net, rope, umbrella, tent, medical bandage, boat sail, fire starter (for smoke signals), blanket, Snuggie, sleeping bag.

Swiss Army knife uses: cutting things (large blade or small blade), can opener, bottle opener, scissors, corkscrew, toothpick, tweezers.

If you were really in a survival situation, don't you think catching the fish would be a priority over gutting it? And what good is a pair of scissors if you don't have any rope to cut? Shouldn't you use your knife in a tent or under an umbrella if you don't want it to rust? And can a Swiss Army knife really make you feel so warm and relaxed while huddling in a tree as a wedding dress Snuggie? I think the winner is clear.

I Am a Domestic God

3

WHEN MY EX-WIFE walked out, she didn't leave me entirely helpless around the house. I had the basic skills necessary to keep myself, the kids, and the house looking decently well cared for. That said, dealing with my own grief and being a single parent 3.5 days a week wasn't easy. I was once the guy who went to work most days when the kids were still asleep and came home to children who had already had dinner and done their homework. Then suddenly I was the one making sure they were getting to school on time, complete with packed lunches and brushed hair. The morning school routine was completely foreign to me: running around my house, throwing together breakfast, and counting down the minutes until everyone needed to be out the door and strapped in for the drive to school. I felt like I was conducting a shuttle launch: "Ten minutes to go! Five minutes to go! Three minutes to go!" There were just never enough hours in the day to do everything that needed to be done. And I was still putting a lot of effort into finding the time and energy to give my children the same level of attention that I always had before. I just did the best I could. Suddenly I was in charge of the cooking, the cleaning, and making sure my kids brushed their teeth. And, of course, I still had to sell boxes.

For a guy who is struggling like I was to suddenly become the master of his own domain, a wedding dress can prove extremely helpful.

TEA BAG

Sometimes when I'm contemplating life, I like a cup of tea. Tea is a perfectly acceptable manly beverage. A wedding dress, not surprisingly, makes a perfect tea bag.

DURING THE LAST COUPLE YEARS OF MY MARRIAGE, WHEN THINGS WEREN'T GOING WELL, I DIDN'T SHARE THE TRUTH ABOUT WHAT WAS GOING ON AT HOME WITH VERY MANY PEOPLE. Mostly because I didn't want anyone to worry, but also in case we worked things out, I didn't want anyone to know about our rough patch. After the split, however, I really relied on the support of family and friends, and a buddy of mine who had gone through a similar experience referred me to a counselor. Because I'm both fiscally conservative *and* a guy, the thought of seeking professional help after my marriage dissolved was tough to swallow. But for the kids, I was willing to try it out. To my surprise, therapy was actually both painless and easy. Maybe partly because of what a comfortable couch she had. And my insurance even covered it, which is thrilling news to any penny-pincher. An added bonus was when my counselor told me that using the dress in so many creative ways didn't make me insane. I appreciated that.

101 USES FOR MY EX-WIFE'S WEDDING DRESS

DRESS USE #17: **APRON**

Have I mentioned how much I hate doing laundry? When cooking for myself or guests, I keep clean by using the wedding dress as an apron. Given its myriad applications in the kitchen, it's usually conveniently at hand.

EVEN THOUGH MY MOM DID A LOT OF COOKING FOR ME RIGHT AFTER THE SPLIT, IT WASN'T AS IF I COULDN'T KEEP MYSELF FED. I'm not really a picky eater. But if I have my choice, I am a meat guy. Give me a steak and I'm happy. When fending for myself, I don't need an oven. I'm content to use the microwave and my grill. I like spending time in my yard, so I'll choose my grill over my kitchen any day of the week. And in Tucson, you can be out back barbecuing year-round. A stovetop is helpful for, say, heating up the water for a cup of tea. But everything else can be grilled. Even broccoli. You simply need to wrap it in aluminum foil. Trust me.

DRESS USE #18: OVEN MITT

A wedding dress makes an excellent oven mitt. Which is handy when you realize you can't feed your children with toaster food alone.

FEEDING CHILDREN, HOWEVER, ISN'T ALWAYS EASY, AND MINE ARE AS PICKY AS THE NEXT. I figured that taking them grocery shopping and letting them pick out some treats would make it easier to introduce new, and possibly healthy, choices. What a proud dad I was the day that they asked for Toaster Strudels. My kids chose fruit! Of course I would buy these healthy and convenient breakfast delights. My pride in my excellent parenting skills was short-lived, with one blog reader commenting that Toaster Strudels are really for dessert, not breakfast. A concerned family friend implored me to stop feeding them to my children; they aren't real food. But the final straw was the night the kids turned down ice cream. In favor of a little toaster pastry. That was it. Cold turkey, we were off those toasty treats.

DRESS USE #19: **COFFEE FILTER**

As you can see, my ex-wife's wedding dress made an excellent coffee filter. Which was great for me, since I could save money not only by making my own home brew, but also on those disposable paper devices. Although you would think I'd get a discount there. I am in the industry.

WHY DO THEY NEED TO SELL COFFEE AT TARGET? I, like most Target devotees, make my own coffee. At home. Because I'm cheap. What I really need is for Target to replace its coffee stand with a cocktail bar. Because when you are a single father and find yourself having to shop for your little girl's underwear, you would really like to have a cocktail in hand when you realize that your only option is to call one of your panty-wearing lady friends (yes, I have *some*) and ask for help. Although standing in the middle of Target, browsing the girls' underwear section while drinking a beer, is probably not going to reduce the number of stares I'm used to getting. I'm not a pedophile, folks! Just a recently divorced dad! Nothing creepy going on over here!

101 USES FOR MY EX-WIFE'S WEDDING DRESS

DRESS USE #20: SHOE POLISH RAG

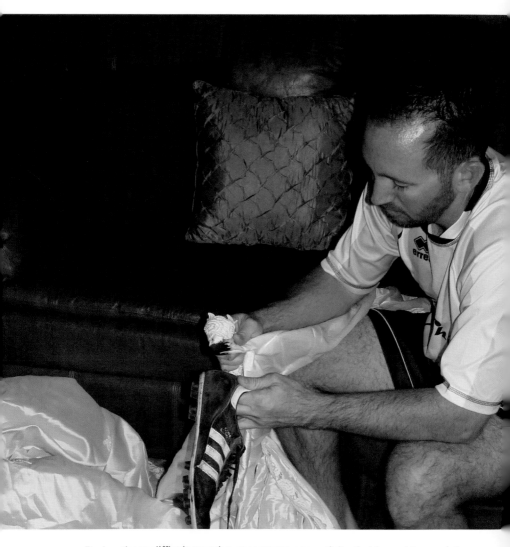

During those difficult months, soccer was one activity that brought me a lot of joy. I love every aspect of the game, from packing my gear to polishing my shoes and even the drive over to the field. Of course, who wouldn't enjoy driving if they had a Honda Element? Anyway, a wedding dress is big enough to polish a lifetime of shoes and works very well, I think.

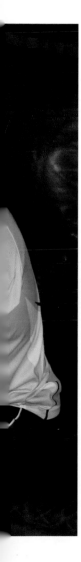

RIGHT AFTER MY EX-WIFE LEFT, I WENT ON A CLEANING AND ORGANIZING RAMPAGE. I covered most of the house, putting things into exactly the places I thought they should go. I had lots of time on my hands and spent hours reclaiming my space. My efforts fell short of the pantry and garage, though. I couldn't deal with the garage right away, simply because my indoor activities resulted in a lot of my possessions being stashed there. I needed more time to figure out what to do with it all. As for the pantry, well, I didn't, and still don't, know what half that stuff is, and I never found the courage to deal with it all. It intimidated me. I decided I would just wait until someone came along who could tell me whether that marjoram should go on my cereal, my steak, or in the garbage.

DISHRAG

I never really like doing the dishes, but a wedding dress makes such a great dishrag that the task feels far more enjoyable. The tulle is really good for scrubbing your pots and pans and getting rid of all the little bits of stuck-on food.

SCHEDULING THE HOUSE AND THE KIDS IS A HUGE CHALLENGE FOR A NONPLANNER LIKE ME. I think I'm pretty organized and responsible, but I don't look weeks and months ahead like it seems most women do. I'm like most guys, I get up in the morning and look ahead as far as going back to bed. Maybe as far forward as a weekend soccer game. But I really need to do a better job keeping track of schedule changes and vacations that involve the kids. I suppose a wedding dress could make a good family organizer if I tacked it to the wall. It could serve as a notepad and a bulletin board. I'll think about it.

JUICE STRAINER

My friend Leah inspired this application. She offered me a jar of prickly pear jelly in exchange for a bit of tulle. I turned her down. However, the prickly pear idea stuck, in the form of a tasty margarita. For those of you who aren't fortunate enough to live in such an exotic location as Tucson, you could opt for a more pedestrian choice, such as an orange, or even a watermelon.

MY BROTHER SAID THAT IT WASN'T UNTIL WE STARTED WORKING TOGETHER PHOTOGRAPHING THE DRESS THAT HE HEARD MY REAL LAUGH RETURN. People have asked me if what I have done with the wedding dress has been cathartic. The answer to that is yes. But not because of the dress. It's because I was doing all this with my brother. We're very close. He even left school to follow me into the box industry. I am still waiting for him to change his license plates to "Box Boy." He did eventually go back and finish his degree, and my whole family is very proud of him. After all, a good education is key to being a successful carton professional.

101 USES FOR MY EX-WIFE'S WEDDING DRESS

DRESS USE #23: **DUST CLOTH**

I was hesitant to post a photo of the dress as a dust cloth, because frankly it doesn't strike me as all that funny. Then again, neither does divorce. There are two things in life that just aren't that humorous: divorce and housework. Although, if you must, a wedding dress actually does make an excellent duster.

EVEN THOUGH THIS BOOK AND MY STORY ARE ABOUT ME AND A DRESS AND NOT ABOUT MY EX, I SHOULD PROBABLY SAY SOMETHING ABOUT HER. I don't hate my ex. Not in the least. After all, we shared a lot of years together and still share two great kids. When my site started getting the kind of traffic that it did, I chose to confess to my ex-wife what I had done before she heard it from someone else. I had to just hope that she would be able to see the lighter side of my shenanigans and know that my intention was not to make my Web site a "bash my ex-wife" forum. But I am not sure if she was more shocked by what I had done or by the fact that other people were actually interested in me and checking out the site. Either way, suffice to say she was surprised. As I'll soon tell you, the worst thing happening in my life at that time wasn't the ending of my marriage, believe it or not. But she took it upon herself to appear alone in court to make sure the divorce was finalized, calling me later to let me know. I would like to think that she was helping to ease my burdens during a difficult time. And for that, I thank her.

DRESS USE #24: **HOT PAD**

A wedding dress is unbelievably useful in the kitchen. It goes from washing dishes to taking hot items out of the oven. Because of its size, it is possible to keep a portion of the dress on the counter to act as a hot pad for items coming straight out of the oven.

EVEN THOUGH MY LIFE IS VERY HAPPY TODAY, I STILL CARRY SOME SADNESS ABOUT THE FAILURE OF MY MARRIAGE AND HOW IT IMPACTED SO MANY PEOPLE I CARE ABOUT. A lot of relationships hinge on that connection between two people, and when that bond is lost, many others are affected. I will never be excited about the complicated child-sharing situation that inevitably comes with a divorce when there are kids involved. I am under the impression, however, that I'm actually lucky as a dad to have my kids half of the time. It still doesn't feel natural and I don't like not having my kids under my roof every night. But they do seem to be adjusting fairly well, and for that I'm very grateful. And I resent the notion that single dads aren't as good as women at raising kids. There are a lot of us doing the job and doing it well, if I may say so. However, I'll be the first to admit that although they go to school clean—clean bodies, clean teeth, clean clothes—maybe I could pay a bit more attention to current fashion. Something I've often wondered is if teachers can tell where a kid spent the night by how sharply he's dressed the next morning. I bet it really threw them all for a loop when Zac Posen and Isaac Mizrahi collections started showing up in Target stores.

101 USES FOR MY EX-WIFE'S WEDDING DRESS

I MIGHT BE A LITTLE OCD

As you well know, I am a Target shopper. Maybe I shop at Target for the same reason I eat at Buffalo Wild Wings on the east side of Tucson— there is nowhere else to go. Or maybe I would be willing to travel to shop at a store that is as tidy. I'm not sure what it is about Target, but just being there feels good. Maybe it's all the pretty colorful items at the end of each aisle, or maybe it's because I can check out in the garden center without waiting in line. My local Target has only one flaw, and that is the fact it has two front doors and one is green and the other is blue. My Target is relatively new, and I watched it go up during construction a few years ago. It was obvious once they painted the front that one door was green and the other was blue. I wondered if they ran out of paint. I struggled with the mismatched doors for some time, but later realized if I park on the side by the garden center I can get in and out without having to look at them.

The Mancave

4

SHORTLY AFTER MY ex-wife moved out, I went through a phase of wanting to establish ownership of all the spaces in my home. When I was married, there were parts of my home that I didn't manage much—certain drawers, closets, and cabinets. I'm a naturally organized person, but I'll admit that when things were going well at home, I was content to overlook these areas. Okay, maybe the inside of my Honda Element isn't the cleanest, but overall I'm a tidy guy. After it all fell apart, I needed to bring some sense of order back to my life. And I thought that taking on the organization of absolutely everything around me would allow me to do just that. Something else that made me feel surprisingly good during this time was decorating. I avoid shopping whenever possible, but I didn't actually need to look outside my home to find what I needed to change the look of my surroundings. My ex had been planning a major redecoration shortly before she left, and many pictures, pots, clocks, and other household items had been stashed in the garage. It may sound weird, but I wanted to put the house back to the way it looked before the split.

When you suddenly find yourself alone and with time on your hands, creating a space that is very much your own can go a long way toward giving you back a sense of control over your life. A wedding dress can really help you make your house a home again.

DOORMAT

Another great use for a wedding dress is to reduce the amount of dirt tracked in from outside. Of course, this application isn't just limited to home use; camper trailers need a welcome mat, too.

YEP, I'M AN INHERENTLY TIDY GUY. I like my house in order. When things are going great, I'm happy to ignore the little things, like those mysterious child-related smudges on the walls, at a height of about two to three feet. If you have kids, you know what I'm talking about. Please tell me that is chocolate. Please. Anyway, in the days after my ex-wife left, I took advantage of all my free time to clean every corner of my home. And then to keep it that way, I simplified my routine; no need to use more than one bathroom when it's just me. And making my bed couldn't have been any easier. I don't move much when I sleep, and when I'm alone I still like to sleep on the edge of the bed, on the same side as I always have. Rather than pull all the covers down at bedtime, I just slid under the ones on my side. In the morning, I just needed to pull the comforter corner back up and presto! All done.

101 USES FOR MY EX-WIFE'S WEDDING DRESS

DRESS USE #26: **DROP CLOTH**

When a man is on a mission like I was, there is no excuse for smudges on the walls of the laundry room. Turns out a wedding dress makes a fantastic drop cloth when touching up your walls with a bit of paint.

LIKE I SAID, I LIKE MY HOME TO BE ORGANIZED. When things in my personal life aren't going as well as I'd like, I take out my frustration by cleaning. I have been known to go on daylong rampages, scrubbing toilets, cleaning baseboards, clearing shelves, and emptying every last drawer in the house. Maybe my car and my office cubicle aren't the most organized spaces in the world, but my home and yard need to be kept in a certain kind of order. Call me neurotic. After my ex-wife left, as I was doing all this cleaning and organizing, in the process I found all kinds of personal items that had gone missing and I'd assumed were gone for good. Take my personalized fishing chair, for example. I thought my ex had given it to Goodwill, but there it was, sitting in the guest bedroom closet.

DRESS USE #27: **RUG**

I'm sure my ex-wife wouldn't have chosen a wedding dress rug for the house, but this is my place now, isn't it?

WHEN IT CAME TO DECORATING MY OWN SPACE, I DI
HAVE TO LOOK BEYOND MY OWN GARAGE. I'm very n
a creature of habit, and since I had nothing against all the s
my ex-wife had staged for retirement, putting it all back m
me feel good. Yes, those Southwestern lizard pots were ɟo
ing right up onto the mantel where they should have been all
along. Of course, I also added some new touches. My ex-wife
didn't appreciate my fondness for roosters? Well, guess what.
That's right. A rooster display. Front and center, I think I uncov-
ered a real hidden talent as an interior designer. It's good to
know I've got choices should I need a career change.

CURTAINS

A wedding dress actually makes a very attractive set of curtains, don't you think? Here you can see that I'm already looking toward the future. I'm really elated that my ex-wife dumped me while I still had hair. I figured I'd need all the advantages I could get.

I HAVE FOUR SIBLINGS AND I LIKE A FULL HOUSE. I originally thought I was finished at two and had a vasectomy. Now I might have a reversal to look forward to, and let me tell you, there is nothing that says "excitement" like having a scalpel *that* close to the family jewels. It's an experience that could satisfy even the biggest of adrenaline junkies. While it's not a sure thing, the odds are good that my plumbing will be back in order in the not too distant future. Nothing I have ever known can compare to the days on which I met my son and my daughter. I would be a very lucky man to experience something as special as that again in this lifetime. The thrill of another child might even outweigh that of a return trip to the outpatient surgery center.

DRESS USE #29: | **LAMPSHADE**

It turns out that a wedding dress is particularly suited to its use as a lamp-shade, because by wrapping or unwrapping layers of material, you can easily adjust the amount of light.

THE AMOUNT OF PLANNING AND PREPARATION IN THE EARLY DAYS THAT WENT INTO DOCUMENTING 101 USES FOR MY EX-WIFE'S DRESS WAS MINIMAL AT BEST. I had enough on my plate without trying to set up Hollywood-style photo shoots, complete with a stunt dress. Colin and I started by staging shoots that required little, if any, equipment or research. However, as time has gone on, the amount of work required to complete my master plan has obviously increased. But I've stuck to my principles when it comes to money. I am a frugal guy. I make my own coffee. And I wasn't about to fork out a hundred bucks for a genuine *A Christmas Story* leg lamp to stage this shot. Of course, if I did, it might be considered an investment. I couldn't find one on eBay, which tells me that this is an item whose value will hold.

DRESS USE #30: **ART CANVAS**

When decorating, you might consider using a wedding dress as an art canvas. I really enjoy contemporary art, and a dress of this size certainly allowed me to express my creativity.

ONE OF THE FIRST THINGS I DID AFTER MY EX-WIFE'S DE-PARTURE WASN'T TECHNICALLY DECORATING, BUT IT DID GO A LONG WAY TOWARD HELPING ME ASSERT MASTER-SHIP OF MY DOMAIN. I took control of my space I made a phone call. And changed my cable television service to DI-RECTV. Complete with the NFL Ticket package. Because it was my first time switching over, the charge was waived, and the package would let me watch every football game, every week. That's right. All the football I could handle. All the time. Right there in the comfort of my newly decorated living room.

101 USES FOR MY EX-WIFE'S WEDDING DRESS

DRESS USE #31: GRILL COVER

Along with DIRECTV and the NFL Ticket, I gave myself a new grill as a divorce present. Had I ordered the cover to go with it, the fit could not have been any better than my ex-wife's wedding dress. If I didn't know better, I would swear that it was actually made with my grill in mind.

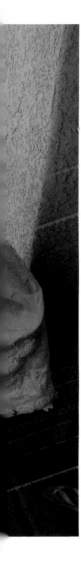

AS I'VE SAID, IF I COULD CHOOSE JUST ONE PIECE OF CULINARY EQUIPMENT TO KEEP MYSELF FED, I'D PICK A GRILL. Every time. To be honest, prior to becoming a single dad, I hadn't actually ever used an oven. Grilling is not only extraordinarily masculine, but it also avoids the obvious risk of burning down your kitchen. My food of choice, when firing up the barbecue, is usually beef. When watching football, a beer and a burger really complement the experience. I read somewhere that the recommended weekly intake of cow should not exceed 300 grams, which is about three hamburgers. I'm counting on that side of broccoli I'm cooking and my mountain trail runs to save me.

101 USES FOR MY EX-WIFE'S WEDDING DRESS

DRESS USE #32: **TABLECLOTH**

A wedding dress makes an excellent tablecloth, both indoors and out. An added bonus would be its size, which allows for it to double as a napkin should you need one.

ONE OF THE EARLY CONTROVERSIES THAT AROSE WHEN MY EX-WIFE'S WEDDING DRESS STARTED MAKING PUBLIC APPEARANCES WAS WHETHER I WOULD WASH IT AT SOME POINT. I will admit that there was an element of guilt in seeing ketchup and mustard stains on a once pristine ball gown after its first outdoor camping trip. And if I'd given the whole thing more thought, I might have changed the order of some applications, such as putting oil pan *after* dental floss. That said, the dress was a symbol of the past, and seeing those first few smears of dirt and food along its shiny body was somehow quite liberating.

MY REASONS FOR LIVING

Another statistic that I discovered while working on this project was that around two-thirds of all marriages ending in divorce involve children younger than eighteen. When my ex-wife and I split up, one thing we immediately agreed upon was that our time with our kids would be shared down the middle, even if that meant we needed to communicate more than was really comfortable for either of us. Neither she nor I would have accepted anything less. But I would like to state, for the record, that my kids' happiness and security, are my number-one priority. Number two is my family and friends, and number three is finding ways to put my ex-wife's dress to use around the house. While a lot of comments on my Web site pertaining to my children were positive and encouraging, that wasn't always the case. A commenter named Susan questioned my parenting skills and the involvement of my children in my project. Are you implying, Susan, that making my kids stand still for thirty minutes to fill out the Darth Vader scarecrow is poor parenting? Just kidding. The truth is my kids haven't been anywhere near my wedding dress antics. I have 3.5 days a week kid-free. Which is plenty of time to put the dress to good use. Every guy has a locked cupboard somewhere in his house where he can hide his personal business from the children. Mine just happens to contain a wedding dress.

I Am a Manly Man

5

PART OF MY recovery after my ex-wife left me was reclaiming my space and making it my own. Initially I wanted to use her wedding dress in the most manly of ways, to show how a dress could fit into a regular guy's everyday life. I like to think of myself as the average heterosexual male. I play fantasy football. I was once chased by a bear. I love nothing more than fishing. That said, I have never been in a fistfight and I can't give blood because I faint. But overall, I like to think of myself as a man's man.

When your wife leaves you, I suppose it is an opportunity to fill your home and your life with all those masculine activities that a married guy might not always have the freedom to enjoy, especially on those days when your kids aren't around. Rather than feeling sad or lonely coming home to an empty house, look at it as a good thing. If you so choose, your home can become one of complete masculinity. You are in control. You want to watch football? Watch football. Feel like eating ribs for dinner? Go ahead. Want to decorate your Christmas tree with beer cans? That's your choice.

At least for a period of time while you are still healing from the split, you have an opportunity to let your inner tough guy really shine. You might be surprised to know that a wedding dress only *accentuates* your masculinity.

HONDA ELEMENT FLOOR LINER

What says "man" more than a Honda Element? That's right. Nothing. And what lines the floor of my Honda Element better than the wedding dress my ex-wife refused to take when she moved out? Uh-huh. Nothing. I'd like to point out that it works not only as a floor mat under my feet, but also as a bed liner when I need to haul my manly tools around.

I DRIVE HONDAS. Period. I'm a Honda guy. I'm also a box salesman, which is why if you are visiting the Southwestern United States, you might recognize me by my personalized plates: BOX GUY. Now I always feel sorry for people who don't drive Hondas. I wonder why they don't just join the rest of us who truly understand automotive greatness. What? You're locked into a lease and have an awesome 100K warranty? Did you read the fine print? What happens if you break down anytime other than between one thirty and one forty p.m. on a Tuesday? You know what they say about something sounding too good to be true. So I'll stand by my Honda. My trusty Honda. You should really think about it.

SMART-CAR COVER

I'm a severely loyal Honda owner. But if I had a smart car, I would use my ex-wife's wedding dress as a cover to keep the blazing Arizona sun from cracking the dash or getting the seats skin-scorching hot. Personally, I think this is one of the cutest applications I found. Yes, a manly man can still find things "cute."

ONE THING THAT HAS ALWAYS BEEN A PART OF FISHING TRIPS FOR ME HAS BEEN CHEWING TOBACCO. I have a fondness for the stuff, but I never dared to use it at home around my ex-wife or children. Of course, when she moved out, I had more evenings to myself and started chewing with increasing frequency. For the first time in my life I was finishing whole cans before the stuff dried up and went bad. And I realized that I was going from recreational chewer to someone with a real craving for tobacco. I now have come to terms with the fact that if I want to have the upper hand and keep my nicotine dependency at bay, I can't chew anymore. Even on fishing trips. That makes me sad.

DRESS USE #35: **SUNSHADE**

You would expect a box man to have a corrugated sunshade. But I also am the owner of a used wedding dress, which fits my windshield very nicely, thank you.

WHILE SHOOTING THE DRESS AS A SADDLE BLANKET, I NOTICED MY COWORKER'S DAD WAS CHEWING. When I inquired as to the variety of chew he indulged in, he told me he'd kicked the habit years ago and was actually using something called "fake chew." Since my addiction is partly ritual, partly chemical, I thought that a nicotine-free alternative would be great for me. That evening I ordered a can, and before long it seemed I had a different addiction on my hands, although I wasn't concerned since it was the "healthier alternative." Then my brother asked me what was in my "healthy chew." I honestly hadn't bothered to look. Turns out it is a mixture of molasses, corn silk, glycerin, water, red clover, ginseng, guarana, and some coloring and preservatives. So now I'm addicted to molasses and red clover. Well, it's a step.

TOWROPE

A wedding dress should be included in all roadside hazard kits. I knew my dress was strong, but this application was the one I had the least faith in as we were setting it up. Of course I knew my Honda was up to the task, but the dress was another issue. I was literally shocked when I was able to pull a Hyundai Tucson for over a mile.

BOTH LEAF BLOWING AND RUNNING ARE IMPORTANT AC-
TIVITIES THAT KEEP ME FOCUSED AND MENTALLY WELL
BALANCED. However, neither can do for me what soccer can.
Not even spending time in my powerful Honda Element can
top it. It's my ultimate release. Not to brag, but I don't suck at
it. I actually turned down a scholarship to play at Regis in Den-
ver. I wanted to stay closer to home and join the club team for
the University of Arizona. I told you, I like it here in Tucson. My
college soccer career resulted in me tearing both my ACLs and
means I probably wouldn't have ever represented the United
States in a World Cup. However, after dropping some weight
on the Divorce Diet—a little program I designed that I'll share
with you soon—I like to think I can still hold my own against
the mostly twenty-somethings I play with. And speaking of
the World Cup, one thing I enjoy almost more than the soccer
is the horns – the vuvuzelas. I like them so much I've thought
about hiring temp vuvuzelas to sit in my living room and blow
during every game I watch. And not just soccer. I think football
and basketball could also benefit from that constant drone. If
it gets to be too much for me, I can always wrap my ex-wife's
wedding dress around my head to insulate it from the noise.

101 USES FOR MY EX-WIFE'S WEDDING DRESS

 DRESS USE #37: **OIL RAG**

I've used my ex-wife's wedding dress to check my own oil, but the guys at Legendary Automotive asked to use it, too, one day. Their expert opinion? Not bad.

AFTER I HAD BEEN WITH MY COMPANY FOR A FEW YEARS, LEARNING THE INS AND OUTS OF EVERYTHING PACKAGING, THEY ADDED JANITORIAL SUPPLIES TO THE PRODUCT LINE. I embraced this new opportunity, and nothing gave me job satisfaction like using the customers' restrooms and then drying my hands on the very same paper towels that *I* sold them. However, while it might seem that this represented a conflict of interest, let me publicly state that I was *never* wasteful. Even though my sales numbers would be positively affected by my attention to hygiene. That would be environmentally irresponsible of me. And while most of my customers offered both paper and hand dryers, I always went with the paper. It's in my blood. Although, if my ex-wife's wedding dress had remained cleaner, I might have chosen to use it instead. At the very least, it makes for an ecologically sensible choice for wiping my hands when working somewhere less fresh, like my garage.

101 USES FOR MY EX-WIFE'S WEDDING DRESS

 DRESS USE #38: # OIL PAN

A wedding dress is large enough to catch almost anything that could drip from underneath a very masculine vehicle like a Honda Element.

BEING A BOX GUY REQUIRES MORE THAN JUST A SOLID UNDERSTANDING OF WOOD PULP AND SYNTHETICS. You need to be a people person, out there connecting with your customers, making sure you are addressing their paper product needs. Of course, the job requires an element of bravery, such as crossing the Mexican border and driving through the tundra to visit, of all things, a *glittery candle* factory. But honestly, what keeps me going, day after day, is the thrill of the job. I can't really explain the rush I get when I take a massive order for plastic bags, or toilet paper, or staples. There is nothing like it in the world. Except maybe leaf blowing.

GAS CAP

A wedding dress makes a so-so gas cap. A video of a wedding dress gas cap, however, is a fan favorite, if the thirty thousand YouTube viewers of this application video I posted have any say.

I LOVE FANTASY FOOTBALL. At one point on my blog I mentioned that my real motivation for this entire adventure was to win a coveted spot in ESPN's Fantasy Focus Football League, run by Matthew Berry and Nate Ravitz. These guys are award winning. I wanted in. They only offer fifteen spots a year. I wanted to be one of the lucky fifteen and thought my public pleas would be rewarded. I'm disappointed to report that while they mentioned me on their podcast, they didn't extend me an invitation. In fact, they only went so far as to *wish me luck*. Jeez. Thanks, guys. What's a guy gotta do? I am seriously betting that neither of them has ever been divorced. Well, odds are that eventually one of them will be able to relate to my story. Not that I'm wishing that on them. No one should have to go through what I have. Not even someone who didn't think I was important enough to play fantasy football with.

DRESS USE #40: PIPE INSULATION

A wedding dress makes an effective way to insulate your pipes, although in a place like Tucson, we don't have to worry too much about frozen water systems.

SPEAKING OF PIPES, I'M REMINDED OF MY OWN. As I've said, when my ex-wife and I thought we were done having children, I had a vasectomy. I'm *that* nice. Anyway, the procedure itself went fine. Snip. Snip. Done. But when the doctor was finished and I tried to stand up, well, that's when I fainted on the table, was fed a sack lunch belonging to one of the nurses, and then spent an hour lying down in the office having my vital signs monitored. Did I mention that the sight of blood makes me woozy? At the time I really thought I was done having kids. And I was. With that wife. But now the thought of a larger family is so exciting that I would be willing to suck it up and go back under the knife. Although next time I'll make sure I bring my own orange juice.

101 USES FOR MY EX-WIFE'S WEDDING DRESS

DRESS USE #41: **CAR WASH TOWEL**

A wedding dress is good for washing your car, but not really great at drying it, as it isn't particularly absorbent. But everything dries pretty quickly in the Arizona sun anyway, so that's okay.

I WAS DEEPLY SADDENED TO HEAR THAT HONDA PLANS TO CEASE PRODUCTION OF THE ELEMENT BY THE END OF THE 2011 MODEL YEAR. With its tough, stain-resistant fabric seats, ability to carry large loads, and easy-to-clean urethane floors, it is a real man's dream car. What is Honda thinking? The newer colors like Fiji Blue Pearl and Alabaster Silver might not be as potent as my 2005 Gunmetal Grey, which is most definitely a chick magnet. I'm not sure what I'm going to do when my beloved means of transportation gives up the ghost one day. I can't imagine life without an Element.

THE FOURTEENTH STATE

The Target Corporation was founded in Minneapolis, Minnesota, way back in 1902, when it was known as the Dayton Dry Goods Company. The first Target store was opened in 1962, and they are now the second-largest discount retailer in the United States. They have plans to expand northward into Canada, and I'm really happy for our northern friends, because they will now have somewhere warm and bright and tidy to do their shopping during the long, cold winters. The people I feel sorry for are those living in Vermont. There is only one state without a Target store, and that is the land of maple syrup. If you use the Target Web site's store locator to find a Target in Vermont, it tells you that the nearest store is in Plattsburgh, New York. I don't think I could live in Vermont. Forget the harsh winters; the lack of a place to shop for my kids' clothes would do me in. At least I now understand why Vermont is the second-least-populated state. Wyoming has fishing, so their claim to the least residents confuses me.

Me Time

IN THE FIRST few months after my ex-wife walked out on me and the dress, I was exhausted. Trying to get my kids to school on time looking sort of together and keeping food in their bellies was truly tiring. Add to that the fact that I was barely sleeping, and I gave little thought to my own appearance or needs. Despite my bone-deep fatigue, however, I did manage to keep running. Maybe it was the adrenaline keeping me going, or maybe I was literally trying to run away. Trail running is something that I've always enjoyed. As the fall approached, I started running more trails, particularly up the Rincon Mountains behind my home, where there are a lot of paths to choose from and some incredible views. Running into those mountains, I had time to process the troubles I had at home, both before and after my separation. Legs burning as I climbed, I allowed myself to think that things wouldn't always be so difficult. I started to believe that eventually my life would take a turn for the better. I would find happiness again. Those hours running were a constant that gave me time to try and clear my head and put things in perspective. After all, I still had my health, my family and friends, and my kids.

In the first few months after a relationship ends, it is easy to forget to take care of yourself, but it is important to make that time, particularly if you are planning on getting back in the game anytime soon. A wedding dress fits easily into a self-improvement plan.

JUMP ROPE

Mastering the wedding dress jump rope takes a bit of skill. I claim to be the world record holder with a total of thirty-seven jumps. I have no need to improve upon that number until I see some real competition out there. One blog visitor claimed to have witnessed ninety-five consecutive jumps, and I asked for videographic evidence. I never heard back.

SUDDENLY FINDING MYSELF AN INSOMNIAC WITH A LOT OF FREE TIME ALLOWED ME TO SPEND EARLY MORNINGS ON MY USUAL RUNNING TRAILS AROUND THE EAST SIDE OF TUCSON. Running mountain trails is so much more enjoyable than just pounding the pavement, I find. While July can be brutal in Arizona, 4:30 a.m. is prime jogging time. I was always a runner, but the combination of waking up alone and waking up before dawn gave me a new level of consistency. Add to that my stress-related loss of appetite, and pretty quickly I whittled off those extra ten pounds I always seemed to carry. Who knew that was the secret? I'm calling it the Divorce Diet, and it will probably be my next book. Watch for it.

DRESS USE #43: **GYM TOWEL**

Another great use for a wedding dress is as a gym towel, especially if your gym mandates that each person bring their own towel and wipe down the equipment after each use. Which is both considerate and hygienic.

SOMETHING I DISCOVERED IMMEDIATELY AFTER MY EX-WIFE LEFT WAS THAT I DON'T REALLY WATCH TV ALONE (WITH THE OBVIOUS EXCEPTION OF FOOTBALL). All the shows I used to watch no longer appealed to me. Which is unfortunate, because I missed out on the final season of *Lost*. I find this particularly tragic because I'm sure they tied everything together and ultimately made sense of the previous five seasons I had endured. What am I thinking? There's no way they could have really done that. Explaining how my marriage fell apart might be easier to accomplish than explaining the Oceanic Six. That might only need two seasons and a miniseries. Anyway, I was able to fill the long and lonely nights by spending a couple of early-evening hours at my city gym. Again, I can credit divorce with my exquisite physique.

101 USES FOR MY EX-WIFE'S WEDDING DRESS

DRESS USE #44: **UMBRELLA**

A wedding dress makes an excellent sun umbrella, which can be helpful in a climate like Arizona's. Sunburn is not healthy. I suppose you could also use it in the rain, although it might not work as well and become rather heavy. Fortunately, that's not really a big concern for a guy living in Tucson.

I HAVE LIVED IN TUCSON MY WHOLE LIFE AND REALLY PREFER TUCSON TO THE PHOENIX AREA. However, I will admit that browsing on Match.com for the state of Arizona leads me to believe that Phoenix might not be so bad. It seemed like there had to be at least fifty times as many single ladies looking for love in Phoenix. Might I suggest that some of them start looking toward the south if they feel they've run out of options for romance? It could be like one of those planned trips where groups of women are sent up to meet lonely men working the Alaskan pipeline. Only warmer.

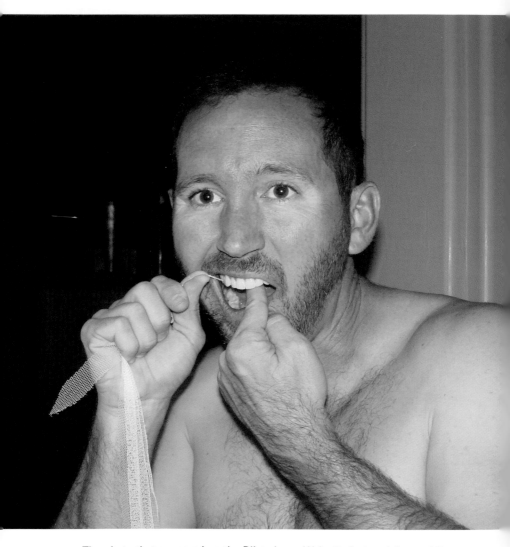

The photo that appeared on the Dlisted.com Web site featured the wedding dress dental floss application. I may have chosen the wrong fabric from which to pull my floss, but I did not find this experience terribly comfortable. And despite what some of the Dlisted commenters suggested, I am not "swishy." Not that there is anything wrong with that. But I want to be clear. I like women.

ONE OF THE AMAZING PARTS OF MY STORY IS HOW THE ATTENTION I WAS RECEIVING SEEMED TO COME FROM COMPLETELY RANDOM DIRECTIONS. I was really proud when *Sports Illustrated* named me their funny Web site of the day. I thought that was a validation of my site's manliness. But then there was a lot of traffic coming from Glamour.com and Jezebel.com—both female-oriented sites. I am still not sure if it was the fashion angle or the feminist political views that I found more intriguing. And then there was the day my mother called to inform me that a coworker had told her that I was the "Hot Slut of the Day" on Dlisted.com. I am sure that she had never been more proud.

101 USES FOR MY EX-WIFE'S WEDDING DRESS

DRESS USE #46: **YOGA MAT**

A wedding dress yoga mat feels so nice on your feet that I wouldn't want to attempt a downward dog without one.

WHEN *INSIDE EDITION* CAME TO FILM MY STORY, I WAS STILL REL-
ATIVELY NEW TO THE MEDIA CIRCUIT. Seeing my living room trans-
formed into a television set was surreal. I had really hoped that they were
coming to film a funny story about a guy finding amusing ways to use his
ex-wife's wedding dress. But *Inside Edition* is apparently not a comedy.
My mistake. I wasn't at all happy with the way I was portrayed on that
show. I am not an angry, scorned ex-husband. I'm just a guy trying to
take a difficult situation and find some humor in it. The one good thing to
come out of the interview was our trip to the yoga studio. I'm not terribly
flexible, but yoga wasn't all that bad. I kind of enjoyed it.

101 USES FOR MY EX-WIFE'S WEDDING DRESS

DRESS USE #47: # BARBER SMOCK

A wedding dress makes an excellent smock for cutting hair, especially a very large one like mine. Colin is a real straight shooter and would never have said that this was the most comfortable barber smock ever unless that was indeed the case.

MY BROTHER AND I CAN TURN ALMOST ANYTHING INTO A COM-
PETITION. Currently we're vying to see who goes bald first. This is one
contest I'd be happy to let him win, and truth be told, I do believe he's the
frontrunner. I have to admit, I was worried about dating again with a thin-
ning head of hair. I personally feel that the shape of my head is not ideal
for a man without hair. I felt that the odds of attracting the ladies would
be improved if I could hang on to what little I've still got. I'm not really
a Rogaine guy, but if there is some other way to delay the inevitable, I'd
like to know about it. Then again, my ex-wife left me when I still had hair.

101 USES FOR MY EX-WIFE'S WEDDING DRESS

DRESS USE #48:  **SNUGGIE**

I always thought Snuggies were stupid but my wedding dress Snuggie turned me into a believer. Try it. You'll be surprised.

THEY SAY TIME HEALS ALL WOUNDS, AND I NOW KNOW THAT IS TRUE. When I started this journey, I was in so much pain, but now I think about those times differently. What has been so healing for me has been the opportunity to help others who are going through the same thing, both personal friends and visitors to my blog. When I talk to a guy who is going through the early stages of a divorce, I tell him to hang in there. I remember how brutal those early days are. Maybe not next week, maybe not next month, but you are going to be okay. And then I say, hey, buddy, if you can keep her dress, do. It's good for so many things.

EVEN BIGGER BUSINESS

My research tells me that the average wedding budget in the United States is around $30,000. Of course, I think that is a ridiculous use of money. But what about celebrity nuptials? It's rumored that Liza Minnelli and David Gest spent around $3.5 million on their little party, while Paul McCartney and Heather Mills pinched those pennies to come in a half million dollars lower. Then there is Christina Aguilera and Jordan Bratman ($2 million), Tiger and Elin ($1.5 million), and Jen and Brad ($1 million). I was shocked to learn that the Material Girl herself only spent a reported $1.5 million on her joyous union to Guy Ritchie, but not as surprised as I was to see that Liz Taylor splashed out twice that on her eighth husband, Larry Fortensky. Is it possible to even begin to defend this kind of extravagance? Okay, I understand that a lot of florists and caterers benefited greatly from the business, and maybe the economy can always use a little shot in the arm. But seriously? At least I can console myself with the fact that all these happy couples are still going strong and will one day be sitting in their rockers on the porch, reminiscing about that great day. Oh. Wait. Right. Never mind.

The New Me

7

I'M A BIT of a joker. Obviously humor is one of my coping mechanisms when life isn't going exactly the way I'd planned. But divorce is something that really isn't very funny. It has a way of making you question who you are and the kind of person you want to be in the next stage of your life. I really endeavored to keep the tone on my Web site light and humorous, even though things behind the scenes weren't always so hilarious. I credit my family and friends for seeing me through those dark days. My parents and two of my four siblings live in Tucson. We're a close bunch and get together just about every week to share a meal and hang out. When my marriage broke up, it affected my whole family, and I knew I wasn't alone in my grief and pain. But shortly thereafter, we faced a different kind of struggle. My father became ill and died just a few months after my ex-wife left. Plans to spend Sundays with my fabulous new NFL package on DIRECTV were interrupted, and instead I sat next to the hospital bed of the finest man I've ever known. I can say with absolute certainty that whatever I do in life, the more like him I can be, the better off I'll be.

Of course, that still leaves a *lot* of unanswered questions about me, although I think I'm slowly figuring it out. I also credit my ex-wife's wedding dress for some of that. A wedding dress can be very good for discovering who you really are and who you aspire to be.

MC HAMMER PANTS

I may have had time to wear my wedding dress MC Hammer pants, but I'm still editing the choreographed dance video. Stay tuned. But I think it looks pretty good, no?

WHILE I FIND THE COST AND THE ABSOLUTE EFFORT PUT INTO A SINGLE DAY SORT OF RIDICULOUS, THERE ARE LOTS OF THINGS ABOUT A WEDDING THAT I *DO* FIND ENJOYABLE; I'M NOT NORMALLY SOMEONE YOU WANT TO WATCH DANCE, BUT I FIGURE A WEDDING IS PROBABLY THE ONE OCCASION WHEN I CAN REALLY LET MY BOOGIE FLY. And then there are the more touching moments marking the celebration. I really wish I could share with you the toast that my cousin Jimmy made at my wedding reception. But I couldn't find the video. You would think it would have been in with all the other reminders of our once happy union that my ex-wife left behind. But it wasn't. Anyway, the point was, Jimmy delivered a powerful and beautiful speech about how marriages in our family last. Our grandparents stayed together. My parents, aunts and uncles have all stayed together. And most of the marriages among members of my own generation—my siblings' and cousins'—were still going strong. He wished for us the same happy ending. Maybe he can find a copy of his speech and repeat it at my next wedding. It was a *really* good speech.

SNOW CAMOUFLAGE

A wedding dress should make excellent snow camouflage, at least when it's still relatively white. I cannot say for certain, however, as I am not a hunter, my gun wasn't loaded, and no small animals were spotted that day. So maybe the camouflage wasn't that good after all.

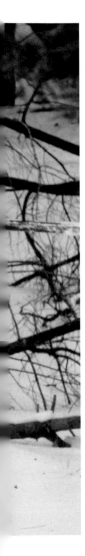

WHEN YOU COME FROM A FAMILY WHERE EVERYONE GETS MARRIED AND THEN STAYS MARRIED, DIVORCE FEELS LIKE A HUGE FAILURE. I know parts of it were out of my control, but it was with shame and embarrassment that I had to face my family after my ex-wife left. I couldn't have been more grateful for the unwavering support I received rather than the looks of disappointment I'd been expecting. Instead of feeling like I had to hide my face in humiliation, I was able to face the world, mostly due to the support of my family. I did mention that free meals are part of the "divorce perks," didn't I? It's not like I wasn't capable of feeding myself, but if my mom wanted to cook for me, who was I to argue? And if I could enjoy a home-cooked meal in good company, well, even better. There is a saying about clouds and silver linings, isn't there?

101 USES FOR MY EX-WIFE'S WEDDING DRESS

SUMO MAWASHI

A wedding dress mawashi actually feels pretty good. I wish I could have found a full-size sumo wrestler to pose for the photographs, but there aren't that many just hanging around Tucson. And after I took it off, I felt really itchy. Maybe I should have washed it after all.

I GREW UP WITH FOUR BROTHERS AND SISTERS. I did mention that my family is Catholic, didn't I? There are families that are Catholic and then there are families that are *Catholic*. As I said, my father was a priest before he met my mom, and after leaving the church he went back to school to get his degree and find a new career. Apparently a PhD in Canon Law doesn't necessarily convey employability. He worked his way up the Diocese of Tucson to eventually become the CEO of Catholic Community Services. He was an advocate for the poor and made sure that his love and consideration of others were reflected in his everyday actions. Despite a modest income, my parents both sacrificed to make sure that we never wanted for anything, even making sure we all had a Catholic education. That's a *Catholic* family. Once again, you can understand why divorce isn't something I really aspired to.

SUPERHERO CAPE

While working out with some fellow superheroes, my wedding dress cape got caught around my foot, throwing me onto the pavement. Which made me look pretty dumb. But not as dumb as Aquaman when he asked the Hulk for some water. Dude. You're Aquaman.

MY DAD WAS IN HIS FORTIES WHEN HE MET MY MOM AND HAD ALREADY BEEN A PRIEST FOR SEVERAL YEARS BY THAT TIME. After my dad left the priesthood to marry my mother, they went on to have five kids. Which means that by the time I was getting divorced, my dad was already eighty-one years old. On September 10, 2009, my dad was hospitalized and diagnosed with cancer. On September 30, 2009, he passed away. Moments later my ex called and told me our divorce was final. I like to think that he was hanging around for me, making sure he could see the situation through. I'm not a big believer in the supernatural, but if that's the case, then it would have been typical of my dad. He's my superhero. And I suppose having spent years studying at the Vatican and dedicating his life to God would have allowed him to choose his time to pass. I guess you could call it professional courtesy.

DO-RAG

I believe that a wedding dress do-rag can make any guy look especially tough.

WHEN MY DAD WAS IN THE HOSPITAL IN THE DAYS BEFORE HE DIED, HE WAS AS UPBEAT AS HE'D ALWAYS BEEN, ASKING THE DOCTORS ABOUT THEIR OWN FAMILIES AND HOW THEIR DAYS WERE GOING. At his funeral, one of his friends said, "No matter what was going on, when Jack spoke to you it felt like you were the only one in the room. You always felt important." The guy who put everyone's needs before his own was more concerned with how his doctor was doing (whose wife also had cancer) than himself. I'm sure he also subjected the guy to the same joke he'd forced upon his own family over the years: "What is the difference between an elephant and a pot for? You don't know what a pot is for?! Ha ha!" My dad had a way of making people laugh with some of the worst jokes ever told. Trust me. When he told it, it was really funny.

101 USES FOR MY EX-WIFE'S WEDDING DRESS

DRESS USE #54: **TURBAN**

My dad made one contribution to this list and here it is. A wedding dress turban will get you strange looks. But it also got me a free coffee at Starbucks, so for a frugal fellow like me, that is a sound success.

I'M A REALLY LUCKY GUY. I have my family and my friends, a couple of fantastic kids, and am looking forward to my future, which hopefully will include more children. I am Catholic, after all. I could not have survived this whole experience without them. Especially my father. He was a strong and gentle man, and I'm proud of him and grateful for everything he did for us. September 30th is not a sad day for me, even with the eerie coincidence of having my father die and my divorce become final at the same time. Because the day he died was the day his pain ended, and it is also the day I could draw a line in the sand and really start my healing. Whatever I am in the future, I had the best of role models.

THE BIRTH OF A VERY CIVILIZED IDEA

After a few scraps of paper and some e-mails had circulated among my family and a few close friends, I had a list of 118 potential uses for my ex-wife's wedding dress. Several of the suggestions from the "original" list were immediately thrown out. I was trying to find a balance between practical and funny, all while doing my best to preserve the integrity of the gown. So pirate eye patch and man thong were quickly tossed. And while I enjoy dressing up sometimes, "plus-size bra" wasn't a look I was terribly excited about. I was also not interested in uses that could get me killed, like sky-diving parachute. I mean, on average more than sixty people die each year jumping out of planes. And that's with a *real* parachute. Most of the other rejected proposals were just dirty, and that's not what I'm about. So puke rag, or toilet seat cover, brush, or paper were out.

While some might find the uses I *did* go for scandalous, I have since learned of something going on with wedding dresses that is far more outrageous than anything *I* could have come up with. Okay, actually, *under* wedding dresses. Have you ever heard of "bride diapers"? No, I don't mean a wedding dress diaper. I mean that there is a whole movement of women wearing adult diapers under their bridal gowns to avoid the entire "which of my friends loves me enough to hoist my dress over my head while I relieve myself of all this champagne" question. Yes, this is apparently a well-known trend among today's young brides. And now that you've heard about this brilliant idea, how can you think my behavior has been anything but completely respectable?

Real Men Do Yard Work

ANOTHER SPACE THAT I put a lot of effort into in the months after my ex-wife left was my yard. I love my yard. It's a place that gives me a lot of pleasure, and I'd much rather keep it maintained myself than pay someone else to do it for me. (Plus I'm cheap.) Although I'm comfortable handling my own backyard, building a Web site and a platform was something I had no prior experience with. Within months of my own divorce, I saw three of my buddies split from their wives, and all three were the dumpees rather than the ones who had chosen to leave. I was witnessing in others a lot of the kind of pain with which I was, unfortunately, very familiar. I really believed that my crazy pictures could serve as a pick-me-up of sorts for guys like us who were hurting. So I did a little research, asked around, and before long my Web site was up and running. After that came a media storm of epic proportions, and the next few months were an absolute whirlwind. It was a lot to take in for a simple guy like me. I had to learn how to be a single dad, manage my home and yard, and at the same time handle my unexpected fifteen minutes of fame.

After a divorce, you have a lot to learn. For instance, a wedding dress can be, surprisingly, an invaluable tool in creating the backyard of your dreams.

LEAF BAG

A wedding dress makes a really nice place to pile leaves and trimmings when taking care of your yard. It makes for very easy transport to the curb or garbage can.

I LOVE MY YARD. It was a difficult property to landscape and required some real engineering to make it work, not to mention a few dollars, a lot of time, and a retaining wall. My dad also really enjoyed that space, and working on its construction was something we had enjoyed doing together. It's really a great yard. Although I admit that I may have gone overboard on the number of trees and small plants. But that just gives me ample opportunity to do what I enjoy most: leaf blowing. There is no chore around the house that brings me more pleasure than blowing leaves. I have never smoked crack, but I imagine that those addicted to it experience the same rush when they light up as I do when I blow leaves. The greatest invention of all time is not the television, the steam engine, or the toilet. It is the leaf blower. Hands down.

101 USES FOR MY EX-WIFE'S WEDDING DRESS

DRESS USE #56: SCARECROW

I live in Tucson. One day without water will kill a tomato plant. I'm not about to let a bird near my vegetable patch. A used wedding dress is scary to humans and birds alike.

I'M A MASTER GARDENER AND A WHIZ AT SALES. I'm not an expert on blogging. At first I just had a little iWeb blog that I'd created on my home computer and gave the address to a couple of friends and family members. Then they shared the link. The initial feedback was pretty positive. Then again, most of it was coming from my mom. Anyway, when I realized I was going to need a Web address slightly more legitimate than my little Mac creation, I looked into getting a professionally built site. Do you know what that costs? If I can't bring myself to fork out five bucks for a coffee at Starbucks, what makes you think I'm about to drop several thousand dollars on something I can't even touch, smell, or drink? But being a salesman means getting to know lots of people. Turns out one of my customers, Greg, designed Web sites for his company. I mentioned my little project, and he was more than happy to help. Greg reassured me that I should focus on the funny photos and just being myself. He knew that I could too easily get caught up in the content, and that could be dangerous; I'm a man who feels insecure about certain punctuation. See there. I used another semicolon. I've learned a lot on this journey.

FROST CLOTH

Winters in Tucson are dreamy. But occasionally the temperature drops below freezing, and when that happens, I use my ex-wife's wedding dress to cover my hibiscus.

BEING OUTSIDE IS VERY THERAPEUTIC FOR ME, AND MY YARD IS A PLACE THAT PROVIDES A LOT OF COMFORT FOR ME. I like it to be kept a certain way because I relax much better in a yard that is tidy. The truth is I'm a little neurotic about certain things in the spaces where I live. Those who know the condition of my cubicle where I work might have a hard time believing it, but I have some freakishly neat tendencies. I really like to experiment with different types of plants in both pots and the natural desert soil around my home. A couple seasons ago I decided to try my luck with tomatoes and other vegetables in a small section of my yard. But my yard doesn't get a lot of afternoon shade, and temperatures in Tucson do tend to stay on the high side in the summer. So I wouldn't say I've been overly successful with that project. But at least I try.

DRESS USE #58: # WOODPILE BLANKET

If you need an emergency blanket for your woodpile, might I suggest a used wedding dress? I think it is unusually well suited for this application.

THE SPEED WITH WHICH MY SITE TOOK OFF STILL AMAZES ME. Within six months of launching my blog, I had received over 2.3 million page views. That's two point three *million*. Some four thousand Web sites out there in the World Wide Web have links back to mine. On the day that fark.com posted a link, my server crashed three times as seventy-five thousand visitors came knocking. Okay, I'm not completely shocked by the local attention, including my cover story in the *Arizona Daily Star*. After all, Tucson isn't that big of a place, and I was walking around town with a gigantic used wedding dress. But to my amazement, the international crowd also accounts for a big share of my followers. A big percentage of the foreign readership comes not only from places like Canada and Norway, where there must be nothing else to do, but also from countries like Germany, where they could instead be watching David Hasselhoff videos and Jerry Lewis movies.

LAWN-MOWER BAG

It's not leaf blowing, but there is a certain satisfaction in mowing one's lawn. By using a wedding dress to collect your trimmings, you can quickly and easily cover a few acres without having to stop and empty your bag, like with those pesky smaller units.

TO THIS DAY, I REMAIN FASCINATED BY THE INTERNET. One of the behind-the-scenes features of my Web site is the ability to see how people found my site. Here is a list of actual Google searches that brought people to me. I am creative, but even I have my limits. I could never in a million and one years make this stuff up.

- I share my wife with my brother
- Can I dress my fish
- How to get a guy to wear a wedding dress
- My ex stole my clothes
- My wife caught me wearing her wedding dress
- Fly fishing wedding
- My wife dresses me like a woman
- Uses for beer to get over my ex-wife
- Husband wears wife's clothes and forced to do household chores
- Women forcing husbands to dress as females

And my all-time favorite? Korean Washcloth.

DRESS USE #60: **CANOPY**

When tied between some of the trees in my yard, a wedding dress canopy provides a shady respite from the heat of the Arizona sun. Shade is essential for enjoying outdoor time in Tucson during the summer.

EARLY ON MY BROTHER JOKINGLY SAID HE WOULD ACT AS MY AGENT IF WE EVER HIT THE BIG TIME. After my blog began generating real interest and I was suddenly appearing on television and radio, my brother visited me at the office. Okay, at the cubicle.

"What's going on?" I asked, surprised at the interruption.

"As your agent, I feel there is something I'm obligated to tell you."

"Okay. What?"

"You need a real agent. You need to fire me."

As wonderful as my brother was at managing my new-found fame in its infancy, he was right. I found a new agent.

DRESS USE #61: POOL SKIMMER

Unfortunately, a wedding dress doesn't make a very good pool skimmer. I tried to clean my neighbor's pool, but I found that it was not only difficult to extend into the water, but that it also became very heavy very quickly.

A BIG CONTROVERSY THAT GENERATED A LOT OF COM-
MENTARY ON MY BLOG WAS WHETHER OR NOT I SHOULD
WASH THE DRESS. It was my brother, Colin, who was so anxious to see the dress lose its perfect shine quickly and pushed
me to go for dirt-attracting applications early on. And I was
determined to see the entire list through without making any
active attempt to improve the dress's condition. However, after
about fifty uses it was starting to look a little ragged, and I had
serious concerns about food safety if I continued to use it in
the kitchen. A good compromise, I feel, were the suggestions
to use the dress in ways involving water that might *inadver-
tently* result in a small improvement, such as a mop or a pool
skimmer.

While I was digging out a damaged drip line in my yard, my wheelbarrow was quickly filled with dirt. Looking around, I realized that I actually had the perfect dirt tarp right in front of me. A used wedding dress makes a great, and spacious, dirt tarp.

SO MUCH HAS BEEN WRITTEN ABOUT MY BLOG THAT IT'S BEEN HARD TO KEEP UP WITH EVERYTHING, ALTHOUGH I'VE DONE MY VERY BEST. It's surprising sometimes to hear myself referred to as "jilted" or "scorned," because this whole crazy adventure has been about finding laughter in a difficult situation. I've learned that I need to keep a closer eye on the kinds of interviews I give and what I say to reporters. Keeping up with what is said about me on the international sites is a little more difficult. My Spanish is good enough (remember that my degree is in business with an *emphasis* in *Spanish*) to make an educated guess that a Portuguese site ran a story titled "Abandoned Husband Destroys Ex-wife's Wedding Dress for Revenge." But when they interviewed me on German television, I just had to hope for the best and assume they were telling my story the way I intended. But for all I know, they could have been comparing me to David Hasselhoff.

DRESS USE #63: **HAMMOCK**

A wedding dress hammock isn't the easiest to install in your yard, but if you are successful, let me tell you that it makes a very comfortable place to rest if yard work, or giving interviews, becomes too tiring.

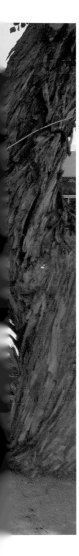

I'VE APPEARED ON TELEVISION, RADIO, AND IN PRINT ALL OVER THE WORLD. I can say that *Today*'s Laura Coffey is probably the nicest journalist I spoke to. Other nice stories were posted on Web sites like Comedy Central's and the Huffington Post. As I saw my public platform grow, I started Twitter and Facebook accounts and now have around five thousand social network fans. But more fun than that has been posting videos of some of the more entertaining photo shoots on YouTube. A picture paints a thousand words, but nothing can convey the heart-stopping terror of stepping into a wedding dress matador cape and facing off against Tuffy the Toro of the Tucson Toros, my local baseball team, like video can. You can also find documentation of something even scarier: the idea of trusting all my weight to a wedding dress hammock. You can actually hear my brother saying, "Commit, commit, commit!" And there is nothing more terrifying to a recently divorced guy than commitment. Of course, some of those 100,000 video viewers were focused less on my feats of bravery than on learning the secret to becoming a world champion wedding dress jump-rope jumper.

101 USES FOR MY EX-WIFE'S WEDDING DRESS

YES, I DO PLAY FAVORITES

I'm often asked what my favorite use for my ex-wife's wedding dress is, and I have to say, hands down it's the Darth Vader scarecrow, which had its moment in the previous chapter. I didn't really have a big bird problem in my garden. Frankly, the Tucson sun is more of a threat to my tomatoes than anything with feathers is. But I had an art easel, a rake, and some mesquite lying around and some time on my hands. Then I stumbled onto the Vader mask sitting in my closet and magic happened. The Vader scarecrow more or less became the symbol for my whole project and is the banner photo on my Web site. Was I trying to make a statement by using the Darth Vader mask on a scarecrow bride that day? Well, maybe I was. I don't really know. One reader said he could imagine it asking, "Luke, does this dress make me look fat?" And that's the point. It's just funny. You already know that I think spending an exorbitant amount of money on a piece of clothing that will be worn once is stupid. And I also think that a Darth Vader wedding dress scarecrow is one of the funniest things I've ever seen. There you go.

Brotherly Love

9

I HAVE SO many people to thank for helping me through the dark days after my ex-wife left. My family's support was invaluable. But the friends who interrupted their busy schedules to check on me were also amazing. Mark, my boss and a man who had once been in my shoes, and Dan, an old high school pal, were particularly persistent in calling and checking on me. I often wondered how anyone could survive such an unsettling time without so much love and support. But I'm not a mushy guy who wanted to sit around talking about my feelings all day. A lot of my healing took place on manly camping and fishing trips. It was actually at my friend Andy's camper that the dress made its first appearance outside its very handsome box, which was at the same time both hilarious and painful. Of course, another source of inspiration was my Web site. When you start a blog, you can't be certain that anyone will actually *read* it, let alone leave comments. However, I included a "Your Story" tab and invited readers to share not only suggestions for my 101 uses, but also their own stories of relationships gone terribly wrong. These stories gave me ideas for the dress and inspiration to keep telling my story, knowing that I really was reaching others going through the same thing.

Hanging out with the guys can be an essential part of the healing process after a divorce. A wedding dress can prove very useful in all sorts of male-bonding activities.

CAMPFIRE CHAIR

A wedding dress in its box makes a very comfortable campfire chair. This is the moment just before I actually opened the box for the first time. If I thought the outside of that box was fantastic, the inside was truly amazing: all these little perfectly designed inserts that fit together seamlessly. It was like a professional box salesman's dream.

THE SUPPORT I GOT FROM OTHER MEN IN THE PERIOD AFTER MY MARRIAGE DISSOLVED WAS PRICELESS. One blog follower warned me of one of the unexpected dangers in being a single father to a preadolescent daughter. "As one who has shared your recent life experience, I warn you in advance of 'tampon purchasing,'" wrote Tom. Not knowing exactly how many tampons his daughter would use in a month and having a deathly fear of toxic shock syndrome, the poor guy had gone slightly overboard on the tampon buying. By the time she went to college, she had enough tampons to supply the entire freshman class (the girls, obviously), even after using them to remove makeup, finger polish, etc. This is the kind of real-life practical advice that a newly single father needs. Thank you.

DRESS USE #66: SLEEPING BAG

I would rate a wedding dress sleeping bag as very effective down to at least 40 degrees Fahrenheit. Possibly lower. I live in Arizona and thus have no way of testing this.

SOME OF MY FAVORITE STORIES INVOLVED THE "CRE-ATIVE" USES OTHERS HAD FOUND FOR *THEIR* USED WED-DING DRESSES. I hadn't thought about making Barbie clothes from an old wedding dress, and it would have violated my first rule about keeping the dress intact (and I'm not really into Bar-bies, but thanks for that suggestion). I particularly liked the one about the guy who cut a heart out of the chest of his ex-wife's dress and sent it back to her. Ouch. And then there was an invitation from Meredith for my dress to have a get-together with a used tux belonging to her ex-husband. I bet my ex-wife is really sorry that I *rented* my tuxedo. Didn't realize at the time how forward-thinking and clever I was being. Just thought it was the fiscally sensible option.

A wedding dress golf towel is effective for cleaning your clubs and golf balls during a round, although I should warn you that a long train can easily get caught under other vehicles, or even your own. Despite the danger, it is still an application that I highly recommend. Using your ex-wife's wedding dress to wipe your balls, well, that just feels really good. So good that I used it as a bowling ball towel, too, and I'm convinced it substantially boosted my score that day.

OTHER READERS SIMPLY WANTED TO PASS ON ADVICE FOR A NEWLY SINGLE FATHER. Whether it is facing your daughter's first period, understanding the difference between Toaster Strudels and actual fruit, or making sure your children have matching socks, I've really appreciated the time that my readers took to help me manage some of the practicalities of parenting alone. I'm even more grateful to those adult children of divorce who let me know that not all children with parents who've split wind up in prison or in rehab. I felt much better. There's nothing funny about wondering if your kids are going to be okay after a divorce. Nothing.

101 USES FOR MY EX-WIFE'S WEDDING DRESS

DRESS USE #70: SOCCER NET

By poking a few holes in your garment and running some cable ties through them and around some posts, a wedding dress can easily replace a traditional net on a small goal.

IF I EVER HAD ANY CONCERNS THAT I WOULD PUT PEOPLE OFF FROM MARRIAGE, I'VE PUT THEM TO REST. My site has attracted people of all types, from the recently divorced to the children of divorce to the happily married and to those actually planning their weddings. But it does serve as a warning to some; an unattached college student named Olga let me know that she's not only already picked out her dream wedding dress but that she's planning on a prenuptial granting her wedding dress a restraining order against her future ex-husband, should it ever come to that. Well, Olga, I have to say, I certainly hope it doesn't.

101 USES FOR MY EX-WIFE'S WEDDING DRESS

By attaching a wedding dress to a couple of tree stakes, it is easy to make your very own golf net at home. I don't know if it was because I could now golf at home or because I was driving balls into my ex-wife's wedding dress that made me enjoy this day so much. Either way, it felt amazing.

OF COURSE, THEN THERE ARE THE COMMENTS FROM THOSE WHO AREN'T AS APPRECIATIVE OF MY WEDDING DRESS ANTICS AS OTHERS. Just to put some of those less-than-positive observations of my story to rest, let me be clear. Dear Catwoman (afraid to use your real name, huh?): I have already been to a professional counselor and she said my antics were "healthy." But I am glad, Ginger, you think the site says more about me than my ex, because it has nothing to do with her. It's my story. Me and a gigantic, formerly white piece of fabric. No, Ken, I do not wish to test how it functions as a noose. And I'm sorry, Pamela. I cannot invite you over to demonstrate that I do not, in fact, "suck in the sack" as you theorize. Although I appreciate your acknowledging that I'm a decent-looking guy with a nice home and an excellent car. And for the last time, everyone, I'm not "swishy."

I COULDA BEEN A CONTENDER

At last count, there are over 150 million public blogs in existence. No, I didn't count them myself. I Googled it. Anyway, the term "blog" is actually a shortened form of "Web log" and can be a personal diary or a way to keep a running commentary on a particular subject, like, oh, I don't know, 101 uses for your ex-wife's wedding dress. It's hard to remember back when there were no blogs, just like it's difficult to recall the days when you had exactly three TV channels to choose from. And PBS, but that doesn't count since they didn't broadcast football. Back to the point. Nowadays, you can find blogs on any subject, from fashion to travel to politics and education. There's even a word, "Splog," used to describe a fake blog whose sole purpose is to send out spam. And, of course, you know if they came up with a word for a Web log and then a word for a fake spamming blog, there had to be a word for a book based on a blog, didn't there? Yep. It's called a blook. You're reading a blook. If only my ex-wife had left sooner, maybe I could have been up for a Lulu Blooker Prize, but those were only awarded in 2006 and 2007. That lucky *Julie and Julia*.

Life's Little Celebrations

10 WHEN YOU ARE newly single, the holidays can be very difficult times. Traditions and family get-togethers are suddenly at the mercy of visitation arrangements. "Dad" time becomes so sacred that letting Granny take the kids overnight feels like she's actually robbing you. But that is really not fair to your other family members, who deserve these moments, too. No matter how miserable you feel, facing a once joyous event while still smarting from the pain of a split, you need to put on a happy face. That's most important for your kids, who are probably going to be very anxious about everything. If you thought convincing your children that Santa could magically find them in the midst of millions of other children on Christmas Eve was hard, try working in their second home address. Of course, they'll get over their fears as they open piles of sympathy presents in several houses on Christmas Day. (Not wanting to fall into that trap, I purposely underpurchased for my kids that first year. Really, it's not just because I'm cheap. It was responsible parenting.) The "new normal" is just a part of life after a divorce, especially when there are kids involved. You have to understand your feelings and work through them. And get over your instinctive possessiveness and share your children with their grandmother. It's the least you could do after all those fine meals she fed you.

Successfully surviving a divorce is certainly one reason to raise your glass and give a toast to the future. A wedding dress can go a long way toward helping you find the joy and happiness in both the holidays and the smaller moments of joy that life brings.

DRESS USE #75: **PUPPET-SHOW CURTAIN**

A wedding dress makes an excellent puppet-show curtain. You could consider a mini Darth Vader scarecrow and a sock monkey as your main characters. The plot is, of course, entirely up to you.

WHEN MY EX-WIFE MOVED OUT, SHE DIDN'T JUST LEAVE HER WEDDING DRESS BEHIND. Oh, no. She left everything pertaining to our holy union: pictures, cards, candles, guest book, you name it. Included in those items was a doll that someone had created in her likeness, complete with an exact replica of her wedding dress. This is no joke. I have a mini ex-wife's wedding dress on a mini ex-wife doll. No lie. I couldn't make this up if I tried. Anyway, a mini Darth Vader scarecrow seemed the obvious use for my mini ex-wife and her mini dress.

DRESS USE #76: **HOLIDAY DECORATIONS**

On its own, a used wedding dress can be pretty scary. But as a Halloween decoration it is positively terrifying. I imagine that with a little creativity, a wedding dress could elevate any type of holiday décor.

I HATE LAUNDRY. I know I've said this a few times. It is a necessary evil, but nothing about doing the laundry brings me satisfaction. What I hate the most is the socks. Where do they go? I have a sock graveyard that is about fifty socks deep in my laundry room and it just never seems to shrink. Once I found about five socks attached to towels and sheets. That was definitely my biggest day ever in terms of taking socks off the pile. It felt really good. I don't remember how I celebrated, but I'm sure I did something special. It wasn't just a good day for me; I was also thinking of those lonely pieces of footwear. I feel sorry for them, just lying there without any purpose. I want to find ways to make them feel useful again. Like maybe stuffing a wedding dress ghost or something.

HALLOWEEN COSTUME

When I used my ex-wife's wedding dress as a Halloween costume, I was going for a caveman look. But everyone thought I looked like Moses. Either way, the good news is that it was large enough to double as a candy sack.

ALTHOUGH I GREW UP IN A VERY CATHOLIC FAMILY, I AM BLESSED TO HAVE PARENTS WHO WERE ABLE TO SUPPORT THEIR CHILDREN NO MATTER WHAT AND ARE THERE FOR US EVEN WHEN WE MAKE CHOICES THAT DIFFER FROM THEIR BELIEFS. After I discussed the annulment issue on my blog, a very nice lady suggested a book on the topic. My mother probably left skid marks in the driveway on her way to the bookstore that day. I know she would prefer that I went through with the process, and I even went so far as to get the necessary paperwork. But then I wonder, upon what grounds could I argue my case? I think anyone who saw me walking around Tucson with a giant wedding dress could rightly argue psychological incapacity.

101 USES FOR MY EX-WIFE'S WEDDING DRESS

DRESS USE #79: **TABLE RUNNER**

A wedding dress makes an excellent table runner, and if positioned correctly poses little risk of actually touching the food. As a bonus, you could consider creating a small teepee with it as a tribute to our Native American brothers.

THE QUESTION OF WHETHER OR NOT I WOULD WASH THE DRESS BEFORE COMPLETING MY MISSION WAS ALWAYS A CONTROVERSIAL ONE. While I liked the idea of seeing what the dress would look like at the end of the process, without any interference from soap and hot water (or wait—is this dry clean only?), I will admit to some initial safety concerns. After a dress is used as a gas cap, is it safe to handle food? However, even toward the end I was able to use the dress as a tea bag and a baby sling. The baby survived and so did the manly tea drinker (me). Leaving me to conclude that the dress may be dirty, but it's not toxic.

101 USES FOR MY EX-WIFE'S WEDDING DRESS

A wedding dress does not make a very good piñata. At least not this particular dress, which I am convinced is indestructible. I think children would be very disappointed by a wedding dress piñata, although it would make for a large target for a blindfolded partygoer.

DIVORCE DOESN'T JUST AFFECT A COUPLE AND THEIR KIDS. There is a ripple effect and friends and family are affected, too. Losing friends is part of what I call "collateral damage," and I suppose I understand how friendship and loyalties can cause relationships to be severed. Those close to me made great sacrifices to make sure I was okay in the time after my ex-wife left. My brother, Colin, was obviously involved in the dress shenanigans, but also spent extra time just hanging around my house. My sister Kathleen dragged herself out of bed and joined me on my predawn runs, which I appreciated. Chatting meant we needed to slow down. Even though she's my older sister, she's still quite speedy and could easily have matched my quick pace, but she was also there to share words of support and encouragement. My sisters Lisa and Amy also checked in from out of town to make sure I was okay. It's good to be a man with sisters. Their attention was extremely comforting.

101 USES FOR MY EX-WIFE'S WEDDING DRESS

AND THE BRIDE WORE WHITE

What kind of wedding dress a bride chooses depends on many things, like her religion, culture, and venue. After all, if you're getting married on the beach in Mexico, a fur collar probably isn't appropriate. (Although it would probably make a very good duster when you got home.) Most Western brides choose dresses that are of varying shades of white, thinking that implies some degree of virtue. But white (or eggshell, cream, or ecru for that matter) isn't the color of purity. *Blue* is. It was Queen Victoria, in 1840, who made wearing a white wedding dress popular. Because she had some lace in her closet that she needed to use up. Okay, so you can argue that a white wedding dress symbolizes a christening gown or the dress worn by little girls at their first communion and has some religious roots. But I know the real reason that the best wedding dresses are light in color: A blue wedding dress would make for terrible snow camouflage. And it would be really difficult for your home team to read your message of support from the wedding dress sports banner (Go, Cats!). Then again, white does get dirty more quickly. Well, I'll leave that decision up to you.

Man's Best Friend

11

AFTER MY EX-WIFE was gone, I found great comfort in having my kids at home and slept much better than when they were gone. There is something very primal about having your young near you at night. When someone who was once your best friend leaves, you return to many basic animal instincts: sleep, eat, protect your young. In that way we can learn from our pet friends. Something else that anyone who has ever had an animal companion can tell you is that not every pet is suited for every person. For example, a chinchilla might sound like a soft and fuzzy addition to your home, but do you really want to hear squeaking all night long or clean up the aftermath of a dust bath? And I know a few people who are probably best suited to a pet rock, to be quite honest. Actually, choosing a pet and choosing a future mate are kind of similar processes. You have to know what kind of relationships work for you when choosing companionship for the future. After all, you just went through a divorce. Of course you want to maximize the chances that next time around will be the one that sticks.

When your best friend walks out, life can get very lonely. You might start thinking about finding new companionship, in the form of a dog, a cat, or even a parakeet. And a wedding dress can be really useful to keep him happy and well cared for.

DRESS USE #82: **DOG BED**

After I kicked Lenny's butt playing wedding dress tug-of-war, I thought it only polite to invite him to have a rest on a wedding dress dog bed. I'm no dog whisperer, but he sure seemed to enjoy himself.

IN DOING A LITTLE RESEARCH ABOUT DIVORCE STATIS-
TICS, I FOUND THAT THE NUMBERS AREN'T ALWAYS SO
CLEAR. In the United States, it is about 40 percent of first
marriages that fail. The eternal optimist, I had hoped that second marriages stood a better chance. Not so. Now we're talking about 60 percent. Third time's not a charm, either, when
it comes to making a lifetime commitment to another human
being. I had really hoped that us divorcés would put a little
more effort into our second go of it. You would think this is one
lesson you wouldn't need to learn twice.

101 USES FOR MY EX-WIFE'S WEDDING DRESS

DRESS USE #85: DOG LEASH

A wedding dress makes a great leash with a loose collar for a larger dog. You'll need to use a lot of dress to make a strong knot, but it is well worth the effort. Lenny seemed incredibly proud to be strolling around the park in a wedding dress leash when I treated both of us to a walk that day.

STUDIES LOOKING AT WHO DIVORCES AND WHO DOESN'T HAVE FOCUSED ON ALL SORTS OF FACTORS, FROM RACE TO AGE TO RELIGIOUS AFFILIATION. Both a higher age and a higher education are associated with a lower divorce rate. I've read that of adults age thirty-five to thirty-nine, those with a college degree are half as likely to be divorced as those without one. But no one has really looked at those who studied business, with an emphasis in Spanish. And I certainly couldn't find any studies looking specifically at salesmen. I think that shows there are some big holes in the understanding of why some couples stay married and others don't.

DRESS USE #88: **ICE PACK**

A wedding dress ice pack is really helpful if you are an aging weekend warrior like myself. In fact, it's large enough that you could actually ice both knees at once if you needed.

ACCORDING TO THE BRIDAL ASSOCIATION OF AMERICA (I KNOW, CAN YOU BELIEVE AMERICA HAS ITS VERY OWN BRIDAL ASSOCIATION? What a nation), the average cost of a wedding in 2009 was more than $30,000. The majority of couples actually pay for their weddings themselves, which means most are starting their new lives together with a mountain of debt. Of course, they could have asked their parents, but is it really fair to expect your folks to pick up the tab for a giant party just as they are facing retirement? And don't you want any inheritance? Maybe a good business model would be a company that specializes in both weddings *and* divorces. Something like "Let us plan your wedding and get 25 percent off the divorces!" Catchy, eh?

SLIP 'N SLIDE

If you are going to use your wedding dress as a Slip 'N Slide, it might be a good idea to call your local paramedic team and warn them to be on alert. I don't even know if you can call a wedding dress a Slip 'N Slide. A more appropriate name might be a Slip 'N Slam.

I'M PROUD TO BE A FISCALLY RESPONSIBLE GUY. And I sort of think that expensive wedding dresses and expensive weddings, for the majority of people, are stupid and wasteful. I'm not a person who has to sit around wondering what to do with my piles of money. I suppose if you are, well then, you can do whatever you want with your cash. But to me, the idea of spending hundreds or thousands of dollars on a garment that will be worn exactly once before being stuffed into a preservation box (although as I've said, the one containing my ex-wife's dress was a sight to behold) is ridiculous. And what is a used wedding dress worth? Well, if after your nuptials you use it as a hammock, a baby sling, a cover for your smart car, or ninety-eight other uses, then it might actually be worth whatever you paid for it.

101 USES FOR MY EX-WIFE'S WEDDING DRESS

DRESS USE #90: DRAG RACE PARACHUTE

If you want to try out a wedding dress as a drag race parachute, then I suggest you find a vehicle faster than a Go-Kart. Or ask a professional, like my brother. He's been test-driving bald for years.

ON THE SUBJECT OF MARRIAGE, I GUESS I'M A BIT OF A ROGUE CATHOLIC. I have no problem with cohabitation without a legally established union. I'm a liberal guy. And I believe that if it is possible for some joker like my brother to get a one-day certification from the state of California in order to legally oversee his buddy Dave's wedding, then we really need to rethink the significance of an authorized union, don't we? I've thought a lot over the past couple of years about what a marriage is. Specifically the wedding. What is the difference between a wedding and a big party? Why are people willing to throw down the equivalent of a down payment on a house for one and serve pizza at the other? Well, I decided that there is only one key difference between a wedding and a regular old party. Chairs. If you throw a wedding, you have to have chairs. If you are only throwing a party, people can just stand around.

101 USES FOR MY EX-WIFE'S WEDDING DRESS

DRESS USE #91: **SURRENDER FLAG**

Due to its size and color, a wedding dress makes a very good surrender flag. I considered actually waving it at a few points during this mission, but I stuck it out. And I'm glad I did.

AFTER MY DIVORCE, THERE WAS A LOT OF TALK (MOSTLY FROM MY MOTHER) ABOUT GETTING AN ANNULMENT. I'm a practicing Catholic, but you would think after all these years of practice, I'd be better at it than I am. I take comfort in its traditions and roots but admit that I have some issues with a few of its principles. Like the annulment. What does an annulment really mean? That I was never married? Twelve years of marriage just gone? Whoosh? The whole thing sounds a bit hokey to me. So I can't get married in the Catholic Church the second time around. So what. I did it the first time and look how that turned out.

MATADOR CAPE

Do you know there is actually a medical specialty in Spain called taurotrau-matologia, which translates to "horn wound surgery"? Being a matador is serious stuff. Your ex-wife can supply the wedding dress matador cape, but it's up to you to find the courage.

WHEN YOU START PLANNING A WEDDING, LOTS OF PEO-
PLE TRY TO GET INVOLVED AND INFLUENCE HOW IT PLAYS
OUT. Some want you to stay close to home, others are looking
for any excuse to fly off to some exotic location. I like the idea
of a destination wedding. After all, you can run off and have a
romantic wedding and then still come home and throw a big
party without needing to rent all those chairs. But there is a
lot to think about when choosing a wedding location. For example, getting married in Mexico isn't all that easy. Not only do
you have to spend several days there before you're allowed to
wed, there is the little issue of a blood test. Mexico requires a
blood test. And that wouldn't work for me. I get woozy. So the
next time I get married, I'm still willing to consider a place like
our neighbor to the south, for maybe an emotionally moving
but legally nonbinding ceremony. Then I can come home and
have a legal wedding in Tucson. Where they don't take blood.

DRESS USE #93: MOSQUITO NET

Nothing says danger like a case of malaria. On a fishing trip on the San Juan, my ex-wife's dress gave me a much-needed break from the intense mosquito population.

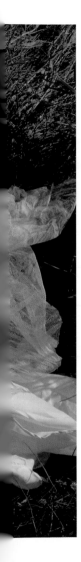

MY NEXT WEDDING IS MY LAST, AND AFTER WHAT I'VE BEEN THROUGH, I COULDN'T CARE LESS ABOUT WHAT I'M WEARING OR EATING. My ring can be platinum, tin, or a twist tie. Doesn't matter to me in the slightest. Even though I haven't really thought through any of the details for my next turn at bat, one thing I'm sure of is that it won't be a big traditional wedding. There won't be any tuxedo, disc jockey, or family members whose names I can't remember. What my bride wears, well, that's up to her. I'm sure after all of this she won't be choosing a big white gown, but if she did, I'd be down with that. No one says you can't be happily married and have a dress going to work around your house. Because there isn't going to be a sequel to this book. Although if she chose to wear a string bikini and I had to, I bet I could find 101 uses for that, too. I'm a creative guy.

PURCHASING SOME PEACE OF MIND

Did you know that you can buy wedding insurance? That's right. If you plan a Winter Wonderland–themed event and an ice storm crashes all the power lines and shuts down road travel, there's an insurance plan to protect you. With the average wedding costing tens of thousands of dollars, it's not an unreasonable decision to buy a policy to reimburse you should a tropical storm, illness, drunk limo driver, or bankrupt caterer ruin your plans. Of course, one thing to consider is whether your chosen policy covers the wedding dress. What if your seamstress dies unexpectedly or a shop fire destroys your beautiful creation of silk and lace? You'll be relieved to know that many wedding insurance policies do, in fact, cover these kinds of unfortunate events. Something else to consider for those planning a destination wedding is whether or not to buy an individual travel policy for the dress. The good news is that most general travel policies cover clothing, but it is still a wise idea to sit down and review the specifics of your chosen insurance with your agent, just to be completely certain that the wedding dress is included.

Back in the Saddle Again

13

LIKE LEAF BLOWING and playing soccer, fly-fishing does wonders for my spirit. My brother and I fish streams, rivers, and lakes. We'll fish in water so cold you lose feeling in your toes for a week. We'll fish from before sunrise until the point when it is too dark to still see our lines. There are some parallels to be drawn between the worlds of fishing and dating. You know the saying about there being a lot of fish in the sea? Fishing of any kind, whether it's for stream trout or women, isn't always easy. You can toss your line into the waters and not even get a nibble. You might feel a tug on your line but reel in an old shoe. As optimistic as I am and even though the thought of not someday being a husband again never crossed my mind, I wasn't thrilled about reentering the dating world. And I live in Tucson, Arizona. There isn't great fishing of any kind around these parts. But I pulled up my bootstraps and got back on that horse, so to speak. And the result is that I'm looking forward to a lifetime of happiness with an amazing woman and our children: hers, mine, and ours (hopefully!).

Remember my wild trip to Starbucks, with a wedding dress turban on my head? I heard a lot of comments that day, but one in particular stands out in my mind. As I turned to go, a girl cracked, "I know one thing you won't be doing with that dress! Picking up chicks!" I laughed at her foolishness. A used wedding dress is not your typical sort of bait (for largemouth bass or female companions), but hey, whatever works.

DRESS USE #94: **SADDLE BLANKET**

I'm no cowboy, so I'll defer to my buddy Jake on this one. Jake's ride Tiny and I gave it a try, and while I felt quite comfortable, Jake said it was one of the finest saddle blankets he'd ever seen. Tiny seemed pretty happy, too.

I RECEIVED A LOT OF RELATIONSHIP ADVICE ON MY BLOG, INCLUDING A FEW NICE LADIES INQUIRING ABOUT MY AVAILABILITY. I was touched and flattered. That would have made an odd "How'd you two lovebirds meet?" conversation at a party. However, there were also quite a few posts, mostly from guys, telling me to run for the hills and never even think about remarrying. But I come from married people. It never dawned on me that I wouldn't one day be attending my own wedding. What my bride will be wearing, well, that is a different discussion. But however I did it the second time around, I had no doubt that it would one day happen.

101 USES FOR MY EX-WIFE'S WEDDING DRESS

DRESS USE #95: **FISHING NET**

A wedding dress fishing net is actually a three-person job, as one must hold the net while the other directs the unsuspecting prey toward his fate. Then there is the issue of the camera. I'd like to introduce you to the first trout ever netted with a wedding dress. At least, that is my assumption.

I CAN CLAIM, WITH CONFIDENCE, TO HAVE STAYED IN OVER 75 PER-
CENT OF THE KOA CAMPGROUNDS IN THE GREAT STATE OF ARI-
ZONA. Family vacations when I was a kid involved two things: a tent and
a fishing pole. I love to fish. I'm obsessed, some might say. I must at this
point declare that, to be clear, no fish is responsible for the failure of my
marriage. After my ex-wife left, I had even less time to indulge my pas-
sion, because suddenly I had my kids 3.5 days a week. I wouldn't change
our arrangement for anything, but having kids around Friday and every
other Saturday night means I have exactly two free weekend nights a
month. Add to that Tucson's happening nightlife and my dating options
looked grim.

101 USES FOR MY EX-WIFE'S WEDDING DRESS

DRESS USE #96: **FLY-TYING MATERIAL**

Although it is a technical violation of the rules, using pieces that are already falling off a wedding dress does create an attractive fly. At least one bass and nine sunfish can attest to that.

TUCSON IS A TERRIBLE PLACE TO FIND GOOD FISHING. To find real trout, I must travel. It was on a trip to Wyoming that I first took up fly-fishing. Fly-fishing is addictive, and it's good that I live in the desert; if I called somewhere like Colorado home, I'd probably be jobless, living out of my van "down by the river," surviving on a diet of river weeds and fish. And also not meeting many women. As it is, I fill my time not on the water by tying my own flies. And what better use for the bits of frayed silk and loose thread that were pulled loose during one of the tougher applications than an XWWD fly?

101 USES FOR MY EX-WIFE'S WEDDING DRESS

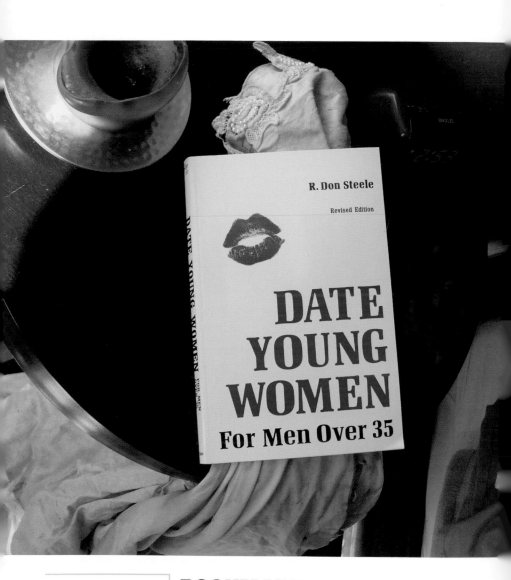

DRESS USE #97: **BOOKMARK**

When I found the perfect book to get me back in the game, I knew I needed a perfect bookmark. Guess what? A wedding dress makes a great page marker.

MY NEIGHBORHOOD CERTAINLY WASN'T GOING TO BE THE PLACE TO MEET THE LADIES. I live in the land of gray hair and small dogs. Retired people and fancy pups. A good safe place to raise kids, but seriously lacking in the single hot women I was hoping for. And as a box salesman, well, you can imagine how many available women I meet on an average workday. I'm not a bartender. I'm a paper man. That left me with Al Gore's Internet. I used to look down at people who used dating Web sites, thinking they must have issues. My sister Lisa mentioned that she thought it was a perfectly acceptable way for people to meet other people in this day and age. Since I respect her a lot, and she seemed to think it was a good idea, I decided to give it a shot. Besides, blue-haired grandmas and Chihuahuas are issues, aren't they?

101 USES FOR MY EX-WIFE'S WEDDING DRESS

PICNIC BLANKET

When you start dating again, it's important to have a list of romantic ways to get to know each other. A picnic is a perfect date. Meet Jessica. I swear I actually believed the doll inside the box would look like Jessica Simpson. After our intimate lunch she went straight back into the box. I hope I didn't hurt her feelings. I know these girls are used to "a sure thing."

MY FIRST ATTEMPT AT INTERNET DATING INVOLVED A FREE WEB SITE CALLED (I'M NOT MAKING THIS UP! ARE YOU READY?), PLENTY OF FISH. Seriously. I created my free account and had a go. Then I realized that no matter how frugal I might be, paying $9.99 a month might be a reasonable way to weed out the carp from the salmon, if you know what I'm saying. I joined Match.com. I found statistics saying that one in six couples married in the last three years met online, and Match.com could claim responsibility for twice as many recently married couples as the second-ranked site. Of course, these numbers came from their own research. But I appreciated their focus on age, height, and relationship status. I decided to overlook the fact that they were missing the one criterion that actually mattered most to me: Does she own a boat?

101 USES FOR MY EX-WIFE'S WEDDING DRESS

KITE

When enjoying a romantic picnic or outing at the beach, consider kite fly-
ing as a way to see how you work as a team. A wedding dress makes for an
extremely heavy kite, I've learned. Did it go as high as the kites of the little
children playing nearby? No. Was it the biggest? You bet.

IF YOU EVER HAVE A CHANCE TO SPEND SOME TIME ON A DATING WEB SITE, LIKE MATCH.COM, YOU'LL FIND THAT MOST RECENTLY SINGLE PEOPLE SEEM TO HAVE TROUBLE FINDING A PHOTO OF THEMSELVES WITHOUT THEIR FORMER BOYFRIEND OR EX-SPOUSE. Their faces were sitting dangerously close to the edge of the frame, leading me to believe that a male companion had been cropped. The lazy ones just blurred the guy's face out. I decided to post one of my own with my ex's face blacked out. Just for a laugh. But that was as funny as it got. Searching the whole of Tucson was pretty unsuccessful. So unsuccessful, in fact, that I actually considered extending my search to Phoenix. If you factor in my opinion of Phoenix, you can see how desperate I was becoming.

101 USES FOR MY EX-WIFE'S WEDDING DRESS

DRESS USE #100: **MOVING BLANKET**

When it's time for you to move on, or move someone else in, consider a wedding dress to protect your furniture. Just be careful that you secure everything well, as satin is slippery.

WHEN I WAS STILL MARRIED, ONE OF MY SINGLE GUY FRIENDS MENTIONED THAT HE SHAVES HIS MAN PARTS WITH A STRAIGHT RAZOR. (We're a tight bunch.) I'm not the kind of guy who is really into "manscaping," but when I was preparing to reenter the dating scene, I thought a lot about that conversation. I took a look. And I broke. Not with a straight razor; that would be dangerous. But I did have some electric clippers lying around for trimming my brother's hair. Or what's left of it. Just kidding, buddy. Different blade. But the first few dates I went on were as awkward as my attempts at self-grooming. I decided I wasn't ready and would back off for a while longer.

DRESS USE #101: JUST MARRIED DECORATION

If you want to draw attention to a new bride and groom, hanging a wedding dress from the back of a Honda will certainly do it. Just in case any of your neighbors have poor eyesight, make sure to include several tin cans and other noise makers to get their attention. What you do with the dress from there, well, that's up to you.

MATCH.COM HAD ME TRAPPED IN A PREPAID THREE-MONTH MEM-
BERSHIP AND I WAS ONLY HALFHEARTEDLY GLANCING AT MY
"MATCHES" WHEN ASHLEY CONTACTED ME. Although I was techni-
cally older than her "upper limit" (at an elderly thirty-six), she appreciated
that I was one of very few men in the greater Tucson area who posed
with his shirt on. That wise decision allowed her to overlook my desire
to meet women as young as twenty-one. At the risk of getting mushy,
I'll say that if I had to make a list of everything I would like in a partner,
that would be her. As an added bonus, she came completely packaged
with an awesome two-year-old little boy. Together we are building a family and looking forward to a long and happy life together. Which just goes
to show what a little ingenuity, determination, and optimism can do for a
guy who one day found himself sitting alone in his living room, staring at
his ex-wife's wedding dress.

The End

SO THERE YOU have it. To anyone going through a divorce, I want you to know you aren't alone. I've been there and it's honestly horrible. But if you can, try to focus on the positive and lean on the people around you who love you. Don't be afraid to get rid of the memorabilia from your wedding, like your ring, your dress, or your ex-wife's dress. Ladies, there are some great organizations out there that do wonderful things with gently used wedding gowns. Guys, if you happen to end up the owner of a wedding dress, I urge you to also consider donating it. But if you're in really bad shape and need some special help, go ahead and break out that wedding dress and put it to good use. I have a feeling that after this, I'm going to see a few of you out there in your driveway, washing your car with a wedding dress that was left behind.

By the way, I want to make it clear that no animals or people were, to my knowledge, injured over the course of this project. Well, except me and those two minor incidents requiring a wedding dress medical bandage. And then there is the issue of my neighbors' roof tiles. During the golf net application, I managed to miss the wedding dress net twice. One ball was found by a neighbor and returned. I'm pretty sure the other one was hit hard enough to clear the houses of my subdivision and reach the desert. However, if anyone living in East Tucson suffered any broken roof tiles during July 2010, I apologize. Maybe we could go shopping at Target together sometime and I could buy you a plant for your garden or something.

To those of you who have followed my blog and the adventures of my ex-wife's wedding dress from the beginning, you might be tempted to double-check the numbering in this "blook" against the dress use numbers on the Web site. Or you might have found yourself wondering why the dress looks pristine in later photos and like a grungy mutt in earlier chapters. Don't. The truth is that the real, chronologically correct history of the dress isn't as important as my story. Call it artistic license, but as I've often said on my blog, the uses haven't always been posted in exact order. Even more confusing, there are some applications on the blog that cannot be found in my blook—they didn't all make the cut. Which actually goes to show that not only are there still many more ways to use a wedding dress that have yet to be discovered, but also that this is one heck of a tough dress.

I also should say a few words about the dress itself. I often wondered during this process: Who made such a fine, sturdy article of clothing? I can only look at my ex-wife's wedding dress with awe; it is a testament to textile strength. A hammock that can support a 175-pound post–Divorce Diet frame? A towrope that pulled a small SUV well over a mile in my neighborhood? Okay, it did scream out in pain (in the form of ripping noises) a few times as we took some turns, but overall it towed that car with no issues. I mean, seriously. A Hyundai Tucson weighs around thirty-two hundred pounds! So who made that fine dress? A company called Jasmine. You should take a look at their site. It's not just wedding dresses. They've got bridesmaid gowns, mother of bride outfits, and even a prom division for your teenage daughter.

I actually sent an e-mail to Jasmine's marketing director and she responded almost immediately, saying that she had forwarded my e-mail to her colleagues and they were having a great laugh looking at my Web site. But I never heard back from them regarding any promotional campaigns involving my dress. I guess I can understand that; it probably isn't great for a wedding dress designer to be associated with divorce. But that aside, the truth is that their products are made to last. I don't know why they go to that effort, but they should be proud. I think it would be okay if they made dresses that fell apart after five hours, because how sturdy does a bride really want her dress to be? And if you want to use your wedding dress as a piñata, I would suggest first making sure that it isn't made by Jasmine, because if it is, well, good luck getting any candy out of there. But I guess this company also views bridal wear as something that should endure, even if the relationship doesn't.

I'm Kevin Cotter. I'm a father, a son, a brother, an uncle, and a friend. I am a loyal Honda owner. I like steak. My favorite store is Target. I'm not afraid to put on a dress but I'm definitely not "swishy." I'm a runner and an athlete. I'm a box salesman with an irrational fear of glitter. And I'm the owner of one very used wedding dress.

But I'm also an environmentally responsible grocery shopper, a prickly pear margarita master, an interior decorator, and a bullfighter. I can use a semicolon with confidence and flair. I took a miserable time in my life and made the best of it. The fact that I come from a wonderful family and they mean everything to me was reaffirmed. And along the way I made a few people laugh, learned just how blessed I am in so many ways, and met someone with whom I plan on sharing the rest of my life. I'm Kevin Cotter and I'm a survivor. My story isn't over yet.

write this book. Under pressure she was amazing, and with deadlines hanging over our heads she was able to make the final stage of putting this all together extremely fun.

Last I would like to thank all the people who took the time to visit my blog and to comment there or send me e-mail. The unexpected bonus of this adventure has been the stories and encouraging notes I received from so many people. A lot of people opened up to me about their own situations and their words were very meaningful to me. I also thank everybody for sending me their ideas for wedding dress applications. I started my blog with a list of approximately 60 uses and would not have compiled the list of 101 uses featured in this book without the ideas from so many people all over the world.

ACKNOWLEDGMENTS

Charitable Organizations

If anybody is trying to figure out what to do with a used wedding dress or a wedding dress that never made it to the big day, please consider these organizations. The links to their Web sites can be found on my blog at www.myexwifesweddingdress.com under the "Donate A Dress" tab.

Brides Against Breast Cancer

www.bridesagainstbreastcancer.org/
Brides Against Breast Cancer arranges national sales of both gently used and new gowns, slips and veils at a significantly reduced price. Their "Brides Against Breast Cancer™ Nationwide Tour of Gowns" sales are an important fund-raising event for Making Memories Breast Cancer Foundation, which is dedicated to bringing joy to those with metastatic breast cancer.

Compassion Connect

CompassionConnect.com
Compassion Connect sponsors the Adorned in Grace project, which seeks to raise both awareness and funds to provide support and safe shelter to both children and teens victimized by human trafficking. Adorned in Grace is a bridal and formal wear shop offering both new and gently used gowns, accessories, petticoats, and veils.

Mary Madeline Project

www.marymadelineproject.org/
The Mary Madeline Project takes gently used wedding dresses and transforms them into baby burial gowns and blankets through the time, talent, and love of their volunteers. These are then donated to hospitals to give to grieving parents. Through their nonprofit efforts, they hope to bring comfort and support to grieving families after the death of a baby.